D1571797

Five Hundred Utah Place Names

Their Origin and Significance

By

Rufus Wood Leigh

Salt Lake City, Utah

First Edition

This pocket book is excerpted from the author's "Indian, Spanish, and Government Survey Place Names of the Great Basin and Colorado Plateaus: Their Origin and Significance."

Manufactured in the United States of America By Deseret News Press, Salt Lake City, Utah.

Introduction

FIVE HUNDRED UTAH PLACE NAMES is a convenient-sized book for travelers and others; it embraces a choice selection from the author's larger work entitled "Indian, Spanish, and Government Survey Place Names of the Great Basin and Colorado Plateaus." The names are arranged alphabetically; each is followed by the county name in which the physical feature or town is located; by reference to the colored map in back of book, the place is easily oriented with respect to county, prominent physical features, and highways.

Under each name, brief, authentic information is given on the geography, sometimes geology, and history of the physical feature or cultural entity. The origin, significance, and etymology of the name are given when applicable. Many place names are comprised of two words: generic and specific; the former is the geographic name; the latter, the particular name, such as *Aquarius Plateau.* A hybrid name is composed of elements derived from different languages, such as *Kanarraville;* the root *Kanarra* is Pah Ute; the suffix, naturalized French.

The toponymy, total place names, of Utah has been augmented and enriched by several disparate streams flowing into the reservoir of geographic names for one hundred fifty years from contrasting cultures including four languages: Indian, French, Spanish, and English. The historical eras and people contributing follow.

Aboriginal natural feature names were realistically descriptive. The Shoshonean stock occupied the Great Basin and much of the Colorado drainage; its subdivisions in Utah are: Ute, Shoshoni including Gosiute, and Southern Pah Ute. The Navajo occupied the region south of San Juan River. It was the wont of the white man to twist, corrupt, and misapply Indian place names; only a few, whose etymology is known, are existent in pure form, such as Shoshonean *Kanab, Panguitch,* and

Quitchupah, and Navajo *Chinle* and *Oljeto*. Short ethnic descriptions of Indian stocks indigenous to Utah, from whose tongues place names have derived, are given.

During the trapper era, 1820-1839, both Americans, mostly from St. Louis, and French-Canadians invaded and exploited the pristine region. The Americans left only their own names on places—Ashley, Henry, Bridger. The French bestowed both personal and commemorative names: Ogden, Provot, Du Chesne, Malade, Portage, Cache.

Prior to and extending beyond the trapper era, *circa* 1813-1850, Spanish explorers and traders from the *Río Grande del Norte* first explored and traded in the *Río Verde* drainage and in the Great Basin; then, in 1829, made the first expedition to *Alta California*. Many other expeditions followed both for trade and for consolidation of Mexican domains. The Spanish Mexicans did not colonize the Great Basin and adjoining Colorado River region, but they left a rich heritage of Spanish place names from *Río Nuestra Señora de los Dolores* on the east to *Río de la Virgen* on the southwest, along the well-worn Spanish Trail between Santa Fé and *Pueblo de los Angeles*.

From the early 1840's through the 1880's there was a succession of exploratory, reconnaissance, geographic, and geologic government surveys through Utah, all of which applied names, particularly to the mountains. Before American sovereignty of the region, John Charles Frémont, under the aegis of the United States Senate, made far-ranging explorations of the Far West and the Pacific regions. He was in a position to promulgate and fix important place names then extant, such as Lake Utah and Great Salt Lake, and to apply others of his own choosing, as Antelope Island. Frémont was followed by Stansbury in 1849 and by Gunnison in 1853, and by a long succession of brilliant and resourceful men, among others: Powell and Thompson, Gilbert, King, Wheeler, Dutton, and in recent times Gregory, all adding richly to Utah nomenclature.

(Continued on back cover)

Five Hundred Utah Place Names

Abajo Mountains are a detached group in central San Juan County; they are an upland from 8,000 to 10,000 feet, surmounted by peaks, Abajo Peak, 11,357, being the highest. The **Abajo Mountains** are laccoliths: masses of igneous rock have intruded between sedimentary beds producing domes of the overlying strata, with subsequent erosion. The word **abajo** is Spanish for "low."

Alhambra Rock (San Juan) is a huge intrusive rock—a dyke, south of the San Juan and west of Mexican Hat, so named by early Spaniards because its contour is suggestive of the medieval Moorish palace in Granada, Spain: **The Alhambra.**

Alpine (Utah). This village was so named because its elevation at the south base of the traverse spur of the Wasatch Mountains affords superb **Alpine** vistas.

Alta (Salt Lake), 9,500 feet, is an old mining district at the head of Little Cottonwood Cañon in the Wasatch. The name is Spanish meaning "upper" or "high." Once famous as a silver-lead mining camp which produced millions, **Alta** is now famed as a skiing resort with its aerial lifts on Peruvian Mountain.

American Fork (Utah) is a stream in a cañon of the same name in northeastern Lake Utah drainage. **American Fork Cañon** cuts through the Wasatch Range north of Mount Timpanogos. The Uté name of this stream was *Timpanogos,* meaning "Rocky River"; the Indians applied the name to both stream and cañon. By extension, the progressive small city, settled in 1850, near the **Fork,** stream, was named for it. The name **American Fork** was bestowed on stream and city to complement Spanish Fork to the south—an older name. The word **Fork** is a generic term for a branch or tributary of a river or lake system. Vernacular usage is frequently erroneous—repetitive, i.e., **American Fork Creek.**

Aneth (San Juan) is a camp on the gravelly point above the junction of McElmo Creek with Río San Juan; **it** is south of Hovenweep National Monument in the Navajo Reservation. **Aneth** has been the site of a trading post to the Navajo since early 1880's. Recently, an inmense, rich oil pool has been discovered and tapped in the valley near here. The origin of the name has been shrouded in mystery. At the author's request, the Rev. H. B. Liebler, Saint Christopher's Mission, Bluff, undertook scholarly researches to determine same; it now appears that **Aneth** is of Biblical origin connoting "fields"—I Kings, ii, 26.

Antelope Island (Davis). John C. Frémont, October 18, 1845, wrote of this Great Salt Lake island: "There is at the southern end of the lake a large peninsular island, which the Indians informed me could be reached on horse-back. I took with me Carson and a few men and rode across the shallows to the island; on the island was found several bands of antelope. Some were killed, and, in memory of the supply of food they furnished, I gave their name to the island."

Antelope Spring, Agua de los Berrendos (Iron) is at the southern margin of Escalante Desert; it was on an alternate of the Spanish Trail and the early Spaniards gave it their name, meaning water hole of the pronghorn, *Antilocapra americana,* fleetest mammal on the North American continent; they still water there.

Antimony (Garfield) is a village on East Fork Sevier River. Prior to 1921, the post office was **Coyote. Antimony** is a tin-white metallic element used chiefly in alloys; deposits bearing the metal are in nearby hills.

Aquarius Plateau (Wayne, Garfield) heads the Escalante River drainage. C. E. Dutton, the eminent government geologist, in his report, **High Plateaus of Utah,** described it thus: "Right south of the Awapa stands the grandest of all the High Plateaus, the **Aquarius.** It is about 35 miles long. Its broad summit is from 9,000 to 11,000 feet above the sea, with Blue Bell Knoll surmounting at 11,253 feet and is heavily timbered with open grassy parks, and sprinkled with scores of lakes filled by the melting snows . . ." **Aquarius Plateau** was named by A. H. Thompson, close associate of Major Powell, on the Second Powell Expedition; its many lakes and brooks suggested to him the concept of its being a "water bearer" — which this Latin word means. **Aquarius** is the eleventh sign of the zodiac. Thompson wrote: " . . cascade brooks made the air musical with running water."

Arches National Monument (Grand) was created in 1929 to preserve and make accessible an area studded with striking erosional landforms west of the Colorado River, north of Moab. The Monument is comprised of two sections: The Windows and Devil's Garden. Name derives from arches formed during long geologic eras by water, freezing and thawing, wind-blown sand, and other agencies of erosion in a 300-foot thick stratum of red rock called the Entrada Sandstone.

Arido Creek (San Juan) is an intermittent stream in extreme southeastern Utah, branch of Río San Juan. The name is a corruption of the Spanish word *aridio* meaning "dry."

Ash Creek (Washington) drains the narrow valley from New Harmony southward to its confluence with La Verkin Creek, north tributory of Río Virgen. **Ash Creek** was so named by John D. Lee in 1852 from the small ash tree or shrub, *Fraxinus anomala,* growing along its banks.

Ashley Creek (Uintah) drains a southeastern area of the Uinta Mountains; it flows southeasterly into the Green River. South of the mountains its course broadens out in **Ashley Valley**, a rich agricultural and oil-producing district. Creek and Valley were named for General William H. Ashley of St. Louis who was the pre-eminent leader during the third decade of the nineteenth century in the fur trade on the Green River, its tributaries and adjacent regions; his was the great name in the Utah valleys in the 1820's.

Ashley National Forest covers crest and both flanks of east-half of the Uinta Mountains. Several peaks over 13,000 feet are in the area. Lakes and streams abound in game fish; a primitive wilderness region is guarded against defilement by man. The Forest was named for General Ashley.

Awapa Plateau (Wayne), c. 8,000 feet, is a comparatively low, monotonous highland, in sharp contrast to the magnificent Aquarius Plateau to its south. The name derives from Pah Ute and was applied by A. H. Thompson. The etymology is: the prefix *A* is locative, indicating place, or place where; *wap* is for so-called scrub cedar; *pa,* the suffix, is a variant of *pah,* for "water"; hence, the name signifies "a stream or water hole among the cedars."

Bad Lands, Mauvaises Terres of the early French-Canadian explorers and trappers—a maze of hills and ravines with almost no vegetation except on the tops of the mesas—constitute a scenery as weird as any on earth. There are typical **Bad Lands** in the Green River Basin.

Bear Lake, lying athwart the Utah-Idaho boundary—northeastern Utah, is one of the larger lakes of the Great Basin. Washington Irving (1843) wrote: "The Bonneville party proceeded down the Bear River . . . and encamped Nov. 6, 1833, at the outlet of a lake about thirty miles long, and from two to three miles in width, completely imbedded in low ranges of mountains, and connected with the Bear River by an impassable swamp. It is called the **Little Lake,** to distinguish it from the great one of salt water." Through usage, the name was changed to that of the river into which it drains—**Bear Lake.**

Bear River is the largest affluent of Great Salt Lake. Its source is at Hayden Peak in the High Uintas from whence it flows northerly into Wyoming; passing Evanston it continues northerly to a point eastward of Woodruff, Utah, where it turns acutely westward into Utah; from Woodruff it pursues a northeasterly course back into Wyoming; thence northwesterly it describes a long loop in Idaho, Soda Springs marking the apex; thence the **Bear** courses southward to cross the Idaho-Utah boundary north of Cornish, and continues an irregular course southward to debouch into the Bear River Bay of Great Salt Lake, westward from Brigham City. Thus, the **Bear River** has three disparate segments in Utah: north of the crest of the Uintas, in eastern Rich County, and southward from the Idaho boundary.

Michel Bourdon, heading a detachment of beaver trappers of the Northwest Company in 1819, pushed south to the **Bear River** and went down it to Cache Valley. Bourdon named it for the bears, both grizzly and black species, which inhabited the region.

Bears Ears, Orejas del Oso, (San Juan) are two knolls near the southern end of Elk Ridge west of Abajo Mountains. The Spanish phrase meaning "ears of the bear" was the name first applied, the elevations resemble the ears of a bear; the Spanish name was Americanized to **Bears Ears.** The pass between the "ears" is traversed by the highway from Blanding to Natural Bridges National Monument.

Beaver, Beaver County, Beaver River. The two former names are extensions of the latter. **Beaver River** has its source in Puffer Lake high in the Tushar Mountains; the main stream is augmented by four forks which drain their west slope. The River flows westerly around the south end of Mineral Range, thence northerly through the Milford Valley to peter out north of Black Rock in Millard County. Before the trapper and pioneer eras, **Beaver River** was inhabited by the industrious fur-bearing rodent for which the River was named.

Beaver County was created in 1856; it is a parallelogram extending from the crest of the Tushars on the east to Nevada on the west. Mineral, San Francisco, Wah Wah, and other Ranges are within the county and are noted for their minerals. One of Utah's few sulphur mines is in the northeast corner. **Beaver,** the county seat, is on the River at the base of the Tushars on Highway 91. The Court House is noted for the historic trial of John D. Lee, a fugitive from justice for many years.

Beaver Dam Wash (Washington) runs southward parallel with the Utah-Nevada boundary, thence southeasterly across the Arizona line to join Rio Virgen. The bed of the Wash is the lowest point in Utah, *circa* 2,000 feet. This stream was so named from occurrence in it of the twig and grass dams of the industrious, well-known fur bearer—the beaver. The generic term *Wash* connotes the dry channel of an intermittent stream, usually the stream bed of a cañon. **Beaver Dam Mountains** bound the Wash on its east; the name of the mountains is an extension of that of the wash.

Ben Lomond (Weber), 9,768 feet, is a peak in the Wasatch front north of North Ogden. This is a transfer name from **Ben Lomond**, 3,192 feet, a mountain north of famous Loch Lomond in Scotland. *Ben* is the Scotch equivalent of "mountain." The peak in the Wasatch was thus named by Robert Montgomery, a Scotsman. Ben Lomond Hotel, Ogden, was named from the Peak.

Beryl is an agricultural shipping station on the Union Pacific Railroad in the Escalante Valley in Iron County. Water for irrigation is pumped from subterranean sources. The word *beryl* is of French origin, the name of a greenish or blue mineral of unusual hardness and beauty; emerald is a variety of *beryl*. The extensive blue heaven of the Escalante Desert may have suggested the name; the railroad has no record of its origin.

Bingham Cañon (Salt Lake) is in the east slope of the Oquirrh Mountains. It is the site of the world's greatest open-pit copper mine of Kennecott Copper Corporation. **Bingham Cañon** was named for Sanford and Thomas Bingham who grazed livestock in the cañon during 1848 and 1850; they also had mining claims there.

Blanding (San Juan) is a thriving small community south of Abajo Mountains. The first village name was **Red Mesa.** This area is historically Spanish, and had Spanish been fully utilized the village could have been named **Mesa Colorado**, and that pretty name might have stood. **Red Mesa** as a name was doomed; it was changed to **Grayson** to honor Nellie Lyman Grayson, a pioneer, but the honor was brief. Thomas W. Bicknell in 1914 offered a library to any town in Utah that would take his name. Two towns accepted: Thurber, Wayne County; and Grayson, San Juan. Thurber became Bicknell; Grayson became **Blanding**—the maiden name of Mrs. Bicknell.

Bluff (San Juan) is a village in the deep, narrow San Juan Valley at the mouth of Cottonwood Wash. **Bluff** was the first Anglo-Saxon settlement in San Juan County. A colony of settlers from Iron County, the San Juan Mormon Mission, arrived at the site of **Bluff** April 6, 1880. After a long and rugged journey over a desolate and broken terrain, they arrived at their greatest barrier: the Colorado River, at a point six miles upstream from the mouth of Río San Juan. Here they found a crevasse leading down to the river and negotiated a most difficult and hazardous crossing. The site has since been known as Hole-in-the-Rock; it will be inundated by Lake Powell. They named their settlement **Bluff** in reference to the sheer banks walling the narrow San Juan bottoms on which they made their home.

Bonanza is a mining town in east central Uintah County. In this district there are extensive, easily accessible, rich deposits of gilsonite, a solid hydrocarbon—a natural asphalt. The word *bonanza* is a derivative of the Spanish word for prosperity; it had much vogue in the Far West for a rich mineral vein or for any venture with an apparent profitable potential.

Boneta is a village in Duchesne County; the name is a corruption of the Spanish word *bonita* for "graceful, beautiful."

Bonita Bend, in the lower course of the Green River, is where two bends come together—the old channel having been abandoned by the river, leaving a great circular rock.

Book Cliffs (Grand) are the lower terrace, below the Roan, of the scarp of East Tavaputs Plateau. **Book Cliffs** were so named because their contours are suggestive of the backs of rows of books standing upright. The upper face of the Cliffs is sheer with talus slopes at base; rivulets have outlined the different "books"; their color is mauve which is most alluring at sunset. The Río Grande Railroad and Highway 6-50 traverse their base.

Box Elder County was organized in 1856; it embraces a very large area of the northwest section of the State, extending from the west spur of the Wasatch—from Brigham City to the Idaho boundary—westward to Nevada. It includes much of Great Salt Lake and the north part of the Great Salt Lake Desert; on the east are the lower course and deltas of the Bear River, the Malad River Valley, and Promontory Mountains.

Box Elder County was named from the abundant growth of the indigenous box elder trees within its bounds. The box elder, *Acer negundo interius,* is native in Utah within the Great Basin. It grows along water courses and attains a diameter of about ten inches. Box Elder is a maple, but it has compound leaves; the flowers come out before the leaves. **Box Elder** and Tooele on its south are the only counties named from indigenous vegetation.

Brian Head (Iron), 11,315 feet, a high point in southwestern Utah, and arising one thousand feet from the plateau base, is the dominant headland of the high Markagunt Plateau. The crest of the headland is composed of upthrust rhyolite fractured by frost action. Visibility from this headland is remarkable. The name **Brian Head** was applied to honor a member of the USGS.

Bridge Cañon (San Juan) drains part of the northwestern slope of Navajo Mountain into the Colorado River; it is spanned by Rainbow Natural Bridge. The Navajo name of the cañon is *Sebige-hotson.* A hot controversy raged as to how the Reclamation Service should engineer the protection of Rainbow Bridge against the waters of Lake Powell.

Brigham City is the seat of Box Elder County; its site is at the base of the Wasatch in the lower Bear River Valley. **Brigham** is an attractive small city in a peach-growing district. The Intermountain Indian School is located here. **Brigham City** and environs are being rapidly industrialized with new chemical and electronic industries. **Brigham City** was named to honor Brigham Young, President of the Mormon Church, eminent leader and foremost colonizer of the intermountain region, and first Governor of the Territory of Utah.

Brighton (Salt Lake) is a resort at the head of Big Cottonwood Cañon high in the Wasatch Mountains: in summer, hiking, fishing, and mountain scenery are enjoyed; in winter, skiing is the mode. The resort centers about a small lakelet—**Silver Lake** which was its first name. Later, the resort was named for Thomas W. Brighton, who built some of the first houses.

Brown's Hole, Park (Daggett) is a slight widening of the Green River Cañon, above Cañon Lodore, in extreme northeastern Utah and northwestern Colorado. This **Hole** was a rendezvous for Ashley and his trappers and traders. In this small valley Philip Thompson and William Craig in 1837 built a hollow-square of log huts called Fort Davy Crockett. For decades **Brown's Hole** was the comfortable, protected home of cattle rustlers.

Bryce Canyon National Park extends from south to northeast parallel with East Fork Sevier River in Kane and Garfield Counties. The rim of **Bryce** is the edge of the eastern escarpment of Paunsaugunt Plateau, 8,000 feet. The drainage is southeastward into the Pahreah River. The several factors of erosion have cut back into the east wall of the Paunsaugunt and exposed the same strata as those evident on the south of the Paunsaugunt and on the west of the Markagunt—Cedar Breaks—all being segments of the Pink Cliffs (Wasatch formation). The name *cañon* is a misapplication of the term: **Bryce** is an exquisitely painted and carved *amphitheatre,* about two miles wide and three miles or more in length, and a thousand feet deep, eroded into the rosy-pink, white, and ochre limestone of the Pink Cliffs; the amphitheatre is studded with an unimaginable number of delicately carved forms—columns and combination of columns; in some places there is horizontal bridging of the columns, all with varying degree of band and pinnacle sculpture. The columns are resultant from the vertical joints in the Pink Cliffs formation. The delicate sculpturing of the sides of the columns is due to the varying degree of hardness—resistance to erosion—of the sedimentary horizontal strata; there is an interplay between the vertical and horizontal action of water in the erosive process. **Bryce Amphitheatre** is a fantastic and bewildering fairyland of enchantment—viewed from the rim or in the depths.

The first permanent settler on the Paunsaugunt Plateau, west of **Bryce** rim, was Ebenezer Bryce, pioneer cattleman, who homesteaded there in 1875. When asked about the cañon to which he had given his name, **Bryce** dryly remarked: "Well, it's a hell of a place to lose a cow."

Buckhorn Spring (Iron), near Highway 91 north of Paragonah, was a favorite water hole for mountain sheep, *Ovis montana,* Paiute *nachi,* and mule deer, *Odocoileus hemionus,* Paiute *tuhu'i.* Moulted horns of the male of these species were abundant here, from which the Spring was named.

Buena Vista (Salt Lake) is a modern Spanish appellation of a railroad siding in the Jordan Valley which means "perfect prospect or landscape."

Cache Valley is the rich agricultural valley in north Utah between the main Wasatch Range on its east and the Wasatch front spur—Wellsville Mountain—on its west. Bear River traverses the northwestern corner. The valley was one of concentration and rendezvous for beaver trappers, 1820-1839. The French-Canadians and other mountain men concealed their peltries and stores in suitable sites in the valley. The word *cache* derives from the French verb *cacher,* "to hide." The noun *cache* was widely current during the trapper era for both the hiding place and the things hidden. Thus, **Cache Valley** came to be known by this name because of *caches* in it. **Cache County**, organized in 1856, comprising the Valley and its watershed, rightfully took the well-established name. By extension, **Cache National Forest** was thus named.

Callao (Cä-yäh-o) (Juab) is a ranch hamlet on the edge of the Great Salt Lake Desert. This place was first called **Willow Springs.** A resident visited South America and became attached to **Callao,** the principal seaport of Peru. Upon his return he had the old ranch name changed to the Spanish name.

Cañon Lodore is that stretch of the Green River's course in northwestern Colorado between the mouth of Vermilion Creek on the north and the mouth of the Yampa on the south; **Lodore** is within Dinosaur National Monument. The River cuts straight into the heart of the mountains forming one of the finest cañons of the Green-Colorado series "where the water comes down as Southey describes it at **Lodore,** and the Major gave it that name" (Dellenbaugh). The literary allusion is to "How the Water Comes Down at Lodore," one of the best known of the shorter poems of Robert Southey.

Capitol Reef National Monument (Wayne) is east of the high plateau country; the Frémont River runs through it. The Monument protects and makes accessible a discrete upthrust of varicolored sedimentary sandstone some twenty miles long. The word *reef,* as here used, is a topographic term denoting an upthrust—a discrete landform with sheer walls. The word *Capitol* was used because the reef's white sandstone domes, topping reddish-brown sandstone, bear a resemblance to the National *Capitol* in Washington.

Carbon County is a parallelogram extending from the crest of the Wasatch Plateau eastward to the Green River in east-central Utah. **Carbon County** was organized in 1894. The name **Carbon** is in reference to the immense deposits of coal and hydrocarbon shale within the county.

Carrington Island in Great Salt Lake was so named by Captain Howard Stansbury for "Albert Carrington, a member of the Mormon community, who was to act as an assistant on the survey."

Castilla Springs, (Utah), **Aguas Calientes** of Spanish America, are in Spanish Fork Cañon. Castilla (cas-tee-yah) Springs were named by the Spanish traders from *Nuevo México* treading the Old Spanish Trail into Utah Valley. They were named for the Spanish Province of Castile, from which pure Spanish flows.

Castle Dale (Emery) is the seat of Emery County. This village is on the headwaters of San Rafael River in Castle Valley. The word *dale* is a poetic or dialectic form for "valley."

Castle Gate (Carbon) is a narrow pass in Price River Cañon. Stream erosion has cut through sedimentary grey sandstone leaving castle-like abutments on each side of the river. As one approaches the entrance, the perspective produces an illusion "of a gate closing." By extension the name has been applied to a coal mine, railroad station, and town near the **Castle Gate.**

Castle Rock (Summit) is a railroad station in Echo Cañon and was so named from a gigantic rock which is suggestive, from its erosional sculpturing, of a ruined castle.

Castle Valley (Emery) extends from about Ferron to Cleveland on the north, at the east base of the Wasatch Plateau, and at the head of San Rafael River. Beds of coal in the Plateau have outcrops on the eastern scarps. The name **Castle** is in reference to the erosional landforms in the valley which simulate old castles.

Cataract Cañon of the Colorado River heads at the confluence with the Green. **Cataract** was so named by Major Powell in 1869 on his exploratory expedition down the Green-Colorado, "because the declivity within it is so great and the water descends with such tremendous velocity and continuity that he thought the term 'rapid' failed to interpret the conditions . . . A large cañon entered from the left (White), terminating **Cataract Cañon,** 41 miles; 62 rapids and cataracts" (Dellenbaugh). Amateur river runners are in danger from the confluence to White Cañon.

Cedar Breaks National Monument, twenty-four miles east of Cedar City at the head of Coal Creek, is a vast semicircular amphitheatre comprised of numerous lesser segments eroded into the western front of the Markagunt Plateau to a depth of 2,000 feet. This escarpment exposes the varicolored limestone strata of the Pink Cliffs of southern Utah, Wasatch Formation. The predominant features produced by the several factors of erosional carving are steeply graded and finely carved myriad ridges from the very rim, which are in groups with ravines of varying depths intervening; at lower levels are radiating horizontal ridges surmounted with partially eroded upthrust walls, buttresses—more resistant strata—below which are talus slopes.

The coloring of the Pink Cliffs exposure at **Cedar Breaks** is at once startling and then inspiring to the beholder: pinks, buffs, oranges, more infrequently rose, lavender. Competent students of coloration have counted over fifty tints. At the rim the elevation is 10,000 feet. The Plateau is trimmed with spruce, fir, limber and bristlecone pine; stunted and gnarled trees fringe the rim; here the rare bristle or foxtail pine (*Pinus aristata*) finds its natural abode—surviving under the most severe vicissitudes.

The name of this remarkable geologic and scenic masterpiece, **Cedar Breaks,** was applied in early pioneer times. The word *breaks* is a generic physiographic descriptive term for a line of cliffs, and associated spurs and small valleys, at a mesa's or plateau's edge or a river's head. *Cedar* is the specific local name taken from that of the town at the mouth of the cañon and creek heading in this amphitheatre: Cedar City. My Pah Ute informant gave the name *Ung Up* for **Cedar Breaks.**

Cedar City (Iron) is the largest town in southern Utah; it was founded November 11, 1851, from the basic settlement of the Iron County Mission at Parowan. The site is below the northwest edge of Kolob Terrace—at the base of the Hurricane fault, at the mouth of Coal Creek Cañon—and affords superb mountain views. It is on Highway 91 and is the railhead of a branch of Union Pacific. **Cedar City** has diversified industries among which is the mining and transportation of iron ore. It is the seat of the College of Southern Utah, Iron County Hospital, and a fine Federal Building; during the summer, it is a mecca for tourists en route to the southern Utah and northern Arizona National Parks.

The community was given the name **Cedar** from the vigorous growth on the site of the so-called scrub *cedar, Juniperus utahensis pinus,* Paiute *wap.* It was a Utah custom to append to specific town names the word **City,** though from many that word was deleted. In this instance the words conjoin well, are euphonious, and remain unaltered; since 1923, the town has had the aspiration and development of a small city.

Chinle Valley, Creek (San Juan) drains into Río San Juan from the south, being a continuation of Chinle Valley of northeastern Arizona. The valley is noted for its prehistoric ruins. *Chinle* is Navajo for "at the mouth of the Cañon."

Circleville (Piute) is a rich farming and stock-raising village on the Sevier River. The root of the name, *circle,* has reference to the circular contour of the small valley in which the village is located; the suffix *ville,* for "village."

Cisco is a Río Grande Railroad station at the foot of Book Cliffs in eastern Grand County. The word *cisco* is Spanish, meaning "broken pieces of coal or coal dust"; seams of coal in the Cliffs have outcrops near here.

Cleveland (Emery) is a hamlet in Castle Valley; it was named in honor of Grover Cleveland, twenty-fourth President of the United States.

Coalville, the seat of Summit County, is at the Junction of Chalk Creek with Weber River at the upper end of Echo Reservoir. The prefix *coal* in the name refers to coal veins in the nearby mountains which were the first deposits developed in Utah; the French suffix *ville* has been Anglicized for "village."

Colorado River, Río Colorado del Occidente, Colorado River of the West, has its source high on the western slope of the Rocky Mountains, twenty miles north of Grand Lake in the Never Summer Mountains; down a steep gradient it rushes southwesterly through Colorado into Utah. At the foot of Orange Cliffs, it has a confluence with Green River. Prior to 1921, the Colorado above this confluence was named **Grand River.** The augmented river with great velocity pours through Cataract Cañon (q.v.) which terminates at mouth of White Cañon coming in from the left, the ferry at Hite is on the right. From this juncture, the Colorado's course is more gentle through Glen Cañon across the Arizona border to the mouth of Pahreah River. Historically, the naming of the *Colorado River*[1] has taken over three centuries—1604-1921. The genesis of the name was that bestowed by Don Juan Oñate in the former year upon the stream now known as Little Colorado River —*Río Colorado,* Spanish for "Red River," because "the water is nearly red." This name was gradually transferred to the *grande* or great river, section by section, finally to the section from mouth of *Río Colorado Chiquito* to the confluence of the Green and Grand Rivers. In 1776, Fray Francisco Garcés, viewing it from the south rim of Grand Cañon, named it *Río Colorado Grande.* In the first half of the 19th century, Spanish explorers elaborated the river's name to **Río Colorado del Occidente.** American explorers and trappers took this Spanish name as a basis for a bevy of variant names: Red River, Red River of the West, then Colorado River of the West. After American sovereignty of the region in 1848, War Department maps labeled it *Río Colorado Grande*—Garcés's name. But the accepted Spanish name *Río Colorado del Occidente* was Americanized to Colorado River of the West which obtained for several decades. At the turn of the century this name was cropped to **Colorado River.** In 1921, publicity pressure in the state of Colorado, whose name was for "the beautiful name of a far western river," secured an Act of Congress changing the name of Grand River to Colorado River.

[1]Rufus Wood Leigh, "Naming of the Colorado River," *Arizona Highways,* June, 1961.

Comb Ridge (San Juan) is a topographic feature west of Chinle Creek, which extends from Arizona across the San Juan toward the Abajo Mountains. **Comb Wash** drains southward from those mountains. "It is a long, narrow ridge with many exceedingly sharp narrow points like a comb" (Gregory, USGS).

Corinne (Box Elder) is a historic town on the Bear River eight miles northwest of Brigham City. It was a boom Union Pacific construction station in 1869. The potential of this site appeared very great: business men, bankers, forwarders, and developers who became suddenly prosperous, visualized it as the metropolis and capital of Utah Territory; in the vernacular, they were mostly gentiles. **Corinne** was an important forwarding station for supplies to new mines in Idaho and Montana; a smelter was built and ores were transported to it in barges across Great Salt Lake from the Oquirrh Mountains. **Corinne** was so named for a daughter of one of the town's entrepreneurs. **Corinne** was a very popular feminine name in that era; it is French, derived from the Greek *corinna* for "maiden." **Corinne** was the name of a famous romance written in 1805 by the celebrated Madame Germaine de Stäel.

Cove Fort (Millard) is a civilian outpost constructed in 1868 on the Mormon Trail, or California Road, now Highway 91, under a directive of Brigham Young, as a bulwark against Indian depredations and as a comfortable way station. **Cove Fort** is on **Cove Creek** which issues from a recess in the mountains to the east and was named from it. A *cove* is a nook in the side of a mountain. In aboriginal times, **Cove Creek** marked the southern limit of Pah Vant Ute territory.

Coyote Creek (Garfield) is a branch of East Fork Sevier River and joins that stream near Antimony. **Coyote** is the name commonly used for the desert wolf, *Canis latrans,* which were numerous in the locality.

Daggett is Utah's youngest county, created in 1918; it comprises an area in the state's northeast corner between the crest of the Uinta Mountains and the Utah-

Wyoming boundary. It has a very small population. With the building of Flaming Gorge Dam in Red Cañon of Green River there is a great impetus in life in **Daggett. Daggett County** was named for Ellsworth **Daggett**, surveyor of the canal to divert irrigation water from Henry's Fork.

Dalles Springs (Tooele) are in northern Skull Valley. The Gosiute name for these springs is *Wánûp;* the composition of the word implies "double spring." The word *Dalles* is French and refers to rapids, running between sheer rock walls particularly, as **The Dalles** in the Columbia River. **Dalles** also means "spout for water" or "trough." The Western Pacific Railroad named a siding, near **Dalles Springs, Delle**—modifying the name for telegraphic purposes. Highway 40, which parallels the railroad, adopted the railroad corruption for a way station.

Davis County was one of the original eight counties created in 1850 when Utah Territory was organized. **Davis** is the smallest county; it extends westward from the crest of the Wasatch, across the narrow, rich piedmont, the salt-marsh land, and into Great Salt Lake to include Antelope Island. Besides horticulture and dairying, **Davis County** is fast growing in industries and Government installations; the County is rapidly becoming urbanized, so that this small county tends to become a large city. The name **Davis** was for Captain Daniel C. Davis of the Mormon Battalion.

Dead Horse Point (San Juan) is the southern promontory of a high, bottle-shaped mesa lying north of a segment of the Colorado River southwest of Moab. Sheer cliffs form the scarps of this promontory. The view of the Colorado Cañon and River is stupendous; this is one of the many photogenic locales of southeastern Utah. The area is a State Park. The name which was applied by early pioneers to this headland of scenic grandeur derived from the fact that a band of wild horses were found dead on the Point; they had been corralled and left to famish of thirst by brutal horse drovers.

Deer Creek Reservoir (Wasatch) is in the stream bed of the upper Provo River, southwest of Heber. The Reclamation Service built **Deer Creek Dam** which backs up the river water; just above the Dam, a north affluent of Provo River, **Deer Creek,** enters, from which the Dam and Reservoir were named. **Deer Creek Reservoir** supplies water for the Salt Lake City metropolitan area via Provo River to mouth of Provo Cañon, canals to the northwest, thence through the Alpine-Draper tunnel under the west traverse spur of the Wasatch.

Dellenbaugh Butte (Emery), near the mouth of Río San Rafael, is "surprisingly symmetrical, resembling an artificial structure. Powell named it for an artist—Dellenbaugh—as it resembled an art gallery." Frederick S. Dellenbaugh was assistant topographer and artist of the Second Powell Expedition.

Delta (Millard) is a well-planned, prosperous town on the Union Pacific Railroad and Highway 6-50. The town is located at about the northeast apex of the extensive region of deltas of the Sevier River above its mouth into the now large pläya—Sevier Lake, dry. **Delta** is the center of an extensive arable section; one of the chief crops is alfalfa seed. This physiographic name is most appropriate in this region of alluvial deposits and fragmented river channel. The term *delta* signifies a triangular alluvial deposit at or near the mouth of a river; this is a special application of the fourth capital letter of the Greek alphabet **Δ**, which corresponds with English *D*.

Deseret (Millard) is a hamlet southwest of Delta; it received this name by extension from **Old Fort Deseret** nearby. **Fort Deseret** was a simple adobe structure built as a defense in case of Indian attacks; it derived its name from **State of Deseret.**

Deseret, Provisional State of. Prior to 1848, the larger region of which part of present Utah is a portion was known as the Great Basin, North America. After the treaty of Guadelupe-Hidalgo, February 2, 1848—ending the Mexican War—Brigham Young organized a potential empire: from the Rockies to the Sierra Nevada with margins of states bordering present Utah and Nevada and extending to the Pacific Coast with San Diego as a port. The **Provisional State of Deseret** obtained legally from 1848 into 1850 when the mirage vanished. Congress organized Utah Territory and the Organic Act was signed by President Millard Fillmore on September 9, 1850. The word **Deseret** is excerpted from the *Book of Mormon;* it is purported to mean "honeybee" and is represented in the central figure of The Great Seal of the State of Utah. The name **Deseret** has been downgraded by wide commercial usage.

Desolation Cañon of the Green River extends downstream from the mouth of Minnie Maud Creek to near the Roan Cliffs. It was so named by Powell in 1869. Dellenbaugh wrote: "Desolation was as silent and deserted as it was desolate and barren."

Devil's Slide (Morgan) is an industrial hamlet in Weber Cañon; it was named from a nearby geologic feature on the mountain side: two parallel, vertical limestone reefs some twenty feet apart, forty feet above the surrounding ground, and several hundred feet in length, forming a steep chute fit for a *devil's slide.*

Dinosaur National Monument, roughly in the form of a large inverted *T*, lies athwart the Colorado-Utah boundary. The Green River makes a grand loop in Colorado in this area; its north-south stretch is in Cañon Lodore, one of the most beautiful cañons of the Green. The southwest corner of **Dinosaur Monument** is five miles north of Jensen—at the crossing of the Green River by Highway 40—on a good highway which terminates at the fossil quarries and a Park Museum. This **Monument** was no named and set aside for the protection of immense deposits in sedimentary sandstone of the fossilized skeletons of several genera and species of *dinosaurs* as well as skeletons of other extinct animals.

The earliest known *dinosaurs* appear on the earth stage about two hundred million years ago; and after a hundred million years of development were in full bloom as to variety of forms and numbers. The University of Utah Geological Museum has several well-articulated specimens of several genera which the public may view. The etymology of the word *dinosaur* is: the prefix *dino* is from Greek deinos, "terrible"; the suffix *saur* is from Greek *sauros,* "lizard".

Dixie National Forest (Washington) encompasses the Pine Valley Mountains with extensions into Iron County and a large area of lower altitude northwest of Pine Valley to the Nevada boundary, including the watershed of Enterprise Reservoir. Much of this so-called forest area is covered with piñon and juniper or brushwood. The major part of this particular **Dixie National Forest** is in Washington County, Utah's "Dixie", so the name is appropriate for this Forest.

Dolores River, Río Dolores, heads in the San Juan Mountains in southwestern Colorado, courses northward irregularly, and crosses the Utah line into Grand County where it joins the Colorado River. The Old Spanish Trail from Santa Fé followed **Río Dolores** for a long distance, then left it to the southeast of Sierra de Sal. The name is Spanish and is a contraction of *Río Nuestra Señora de los Dolores,* "River of our Lady of Sorrows", referring to The Virgin.

Duchesne River, by extension, **Fort Duchesne, Duchesne,** and **Duchesne County.** The River heads in the southwesterly reaches of the High Uintas; the originating forks are gathered to flow rapidly eastward to a confluence with the Uinta River and thence southeasterly to debouch into the Green River near Ouray. **Fort Duchesne** is a short distance above the mouth of the Uinta; it was an early trading post; later, it was used by the Indian Service and was a military post. **Duchesne,** the county seat, is a modern, thriving town on Highway 40 at the confluence of Strawberry River with the Duchesne. **Duchesne County** embraces a large squarish region extending southward from the crest of the Uinta Mountains to join Carbon County on its south.

The name **Duchesne** is an American modification of a French surname, **Du Chesne** (du-shayne). A trapper named **Du Chesne** appears to have headquartered in the Uinta Basin *circa* 1840, and the River may have been named for him. However, Father De Smet may have been instrumental in naming the River in honor of Rose **Du Chesne,** founder in America of the Society of the Sacred Heart, who came from a prominent French family of St. Charles, Missouri.

Dutch John is the name of Flaming Gorge Dam townsite, two miles northeast of the dam. This is a planned town to house construction workers, later, operators of the dam and hydroelectric plant. **Dutch John** is a contraction of **Dutch John Flats,** the name of the terrain on which the town is located. This name derives from "Dutch" John Hanselena, a horse trader and miner from Schleswig, Prussia, who settled on the Red Cañon bottoms in early 1860's.

Echo Cañon (Summit) is a strategic defile into the Wasatch Mountains from over the summit just west of the Utah-Wyoming boundary; in it is a north fork of Weber River joining at **Echo,** a railroad station. This entrance into the Wasatch Range was the route of the Donner-Reed party from Fort Bridger thence via East Cañon into the Salt Lake Valley in 1846; the Mormon pioneers followed this trail blazed by the Donner party in 1847; it became an optional route for California immigrants instead of the longer road via Fort Hall. The Union Pacific Railroad laid their tracks down it in 1867, thence followed the Weber River to Ogden; and the rail route became that of Highway 30 South. **Echo's** walls sharply reflect sound waves, hence the name.

Echo Park, Pat's Hole (Dinosaur N.M.), is a small open valley at the south end of Cañon Lodore where the Yampa River, coming in from the east, has a confluence with the Green in Colorado. The Second Powell expedition in 1871 had called this small valley **Echo Park** from its tendency to re-echo sound waves. Earlier, it had been known as **Pat's Hole** and was a hideout for cattle rustlers. In the early 1950's, the Bureau of Reclamation planned a Colorado River storage reservoir to fill this valley. **Echo Park** is within Dinosaur National Monument; because of this and otherwise, a bitter national propaganda campaign was waged against construction of **Echo Park Dam.** The Reclamation Service substituted Flaming Gorge Dam upstream.

Elsinore (Sevier) is a farming village on Highway 89; it was named from **Elsinore**, Denmark. **Elsinore** was settled by Mormon immigrants from that seaport.

El Vado de los Padres, The Crossing of the Fathers, is a Colorado River ford a few miles north of the Utah-Arizona boundary and fourteen miles above Glen Cañon Dam. It will be inundated by Lake Powell. On November 7, 1776, the Dominguez-Escalante expedition found this old Ute ford. *Los padres* had abandoned their plan of exploring an overland route to Monterey in *Alta California* and suffered extreme hardship in locating a crossing of Río Colorado on their return to *Nuevo Mexico.* This ford had doubtless been known to aborigines for centuries, but this Spanish party were the first Europeans to negotiate the turbulent Colorado. Antonio Armijo was next to cross here on his expedition from Abiquiu, *Nuevo Mexico,* to the *Mission de San Gabriel* in November, 1829, and again on his return with a *remuda* of large California mules. It is a good passable ford more than a mile in width during low water; horses do not have to swim. In commemoration of the first crossing, it became known to the Spanish as *El Vada de los Padres;* after American sovereignty of the region the name was Anglicized.

Emery County is an immense region south of Carbon County extending from the Wasatch Plateau eastward to the Green River; it was organized in 1880. **Emery County** was named in honor of George W. Emery, Territorial Governor 1875-1880. "Castle County" was first proposed as the name from Castle Valley which parallels the Plateau on its east.

Enoch (Iron) is a hamlet at the west base of the Summit ridge; here a sparkling spring wells from a basaltic ledge which waters a lush meadow. The Escalante party came southward this way from the Escalante Desert in 1776. Mormons from Parowan settled at this spring in the 1850's; they named their favored homestead after the Biblical **Enoch**: A patriarch who "walked with God" (Genesis 5:24).

Enterprise (Washington) is a farming village on the edge of Escalante Desert which was settled in 1895. Previously, the founders had lived in the hamlet of Hebron higher up in the narrow Shoal Creek valley. By abandoning their first homes, the ranch people were enabled to build the **Enterprise Reservoir,** conserve the Shoal Creek water, and canalize it onto the broad, rich alluvial plain. This was an enterprising project; so, the new town seemed worthy of the name **Enterprise.** The **Reservoir** is one of Utah's choice fishing lakes.

Escalante Desert (Iron) is a vast, nearly level stretch with an elevation of 5,000 feet, extending from southern Beaver County across Iron in a southwesterly direction and comprising the west half of Iron. During the ice age, **Escalante Desert** was covered by an extended arm of extinct Lake Bonneville; Table Butte south of Lund was an islet in this bay. Climate of the area is notable for warm to hot days with a sharp drop in temperature at night. Mirages are frequently seen in summer. This terrain is the habitat of the pronghorn, the jack rabbit, and the coyote.

Escalante Desert was named for Fray Francisco Silvestre de **Escalante,** leader of the Dominguez-Escalante expedition from Santa Fe in 1776—the first Europeans in the Great Basin. Their route southward from Lake Utah was almost identical with the present Union Pacific Railroad until they reached a point about ten miles south of Nada. Here, abandonment of their objective, faraway Monterey, *Alta California,* is manifest—they turned sharply southeastward to present Enoch.

Escalante (Garfield) is a ranch town on the upper reaches of Escalante River; its name derives from that of the river, a frequent pattern of place naming.

Escalante River is in the barren rock region west of the Colorado River, draining southeasterly through Garfield and Kane Counties. A. H. Thompson of the Second Powell expedition in 1871-72 on his overland journey to the Unknown (Henry) Mountains named this river "in honor of Father Escalante, the old Spanish explorer." *Fray de Escalante* forded the Colorado downstream in Glen Cañon, forty miles from the mouth of the **Escalante River.**

Eureka (Juab), 6,396, is an historic mining town, center of the Tintic Mining District. Several western mining states have their **Eurekas.** The word is of Greek origin signifying "I have found (it)!—an exclamation in the vernacular of prospectors connoting "I have found the lode or vein of precious mineral."

Fayette (San Pete) is a hamlet near the upper end of Sevier Bridge Reservoir. The name refers to Mormon history, and also represents a common custom of transferring names from one section of the country or world to another. The name is a transfer from **Fayette,** Seneca County, New York, where the Mormon Church was founded by Joseph Smith on April 6, 1830.

Ferron (Emery), a village south of Castle Dale, was named for A. D. **Ferron,** original surveyor of Emery and Carbon counties.

Fillmore is the county seat of Millard and both were named for President Millard Fillmore who signed the Act creating the Territory of Utah, September 9, 1850. **Fillmore** is situated on the western piedmont of Pah Vant Plateau; it was the Territory's first Capital, and the old State House has been preserved as an historical museum and park.

Fish Lake (Sevier) is in the mountains east of Koosharem. From time unknown this lake has been prolific in native fish for which it was named. The Pavogowunsin Utes were heavily dependent upon its fish for sustenance. C. E. Dutton in his geologic and beautiful descriptions of the High Plateaus of Utah wrote: "The next member southward is the **Fish Lake Plateau;** it is small in area, but lofty and is a true table. Its southeastern escarpment looks down into a profound depression in which rests a beautiful lake." "**Fish Lake** is 8,600 feet above the sea, between mountain walls, the crystal-clear expanse of the lake combine to form a scene of beauty rarely equaled in the Far West."

Flaming Gorge (Daggett) is the first of the Green-Colorado series of cañons; the entrance to this remarkable gorge is three miles south of the Utah-Wyoming line on the north flank of the Uinta Mountains. At the foot of the level Green River Valley the River has carved a gap into the solid west-east wall. Geologically, it is not easily explicable just how the stream eroded an entrance—to be denied further southern course. Clearing Bear Mountain at a right angle, the river is diverted due east into Red Cañon. Dellenbaugh describes the gorge and circumstance of naming: ". . . the boats proceeded toward a high spur of the Uintas, directly in front of us . . . we could see high up before us some bright red rocks . . . From these bright rocks glowing in the sunlight like a flame above the grey-green of the ridge, the Major had bestowed the name **Flaming Gorge.**"

Flaming Gorge Dam is to be a 490-foot-high, sharply curved, concrete structure across the Green River channel in Red Cañon, twenty-eight miles downstream from **Flaming Gorge** from which name that of the dam is taken. The Dam will back up the waters of Green River ninety-one miles in **Flaming Gorge Reservoir**—to a point a few miles downstream from Green River, Wyoming.

Fort Douglas is situated on the Provo terrace of Lake Bonneville contiguous with Salt Lake City on the east. On October 24, 1862, Colonel Patrick E. Connor, in command of the Third California Infantry, was ordered to Utah and upon arrival established his Headquarters on the east bench. He named the post **Camp Douglas**

for Senator Stephen A. Douglas of Illinois, then a leader in the Senate. Since War II, much the larger area of **Fort Douglas** has been transferred to the University of Utah and others.

Fort Uintah (Uintah), just above the confluence of the Uinta and White Rocks Rivers, near the present site of White Rocks, was established in 1832 by Antoine Roubidoux, a trapper and fur trader of French descent. This was the first white settlement in Utah, called **Robidoux** sometimes.

Four Corners is in the San Juan Valley. Here four states meet at a common point, the only place in the United States where such occurs: Utah, Colorado, New Mexico, and Arizona. This point is probably not far from the center of the highest aboriginal culture in the United States.

Frémont (Wayne) is a hamlet on the upper reaches of Frémont River. All the villages in Wayne County are in the narrow valley of the Frémont. This hamlet was given the name of the river on whose banks it is located.

Frémont Island, in Great Salt Lake opposite the mouth of Weber River, was explored by Captain John C. Frémont on September 9, 1843: " . we ascended to the highest point of the island—a bare rocky peak, 800 feet above the lake. . . on which there is neither water nor trees . . In the first disappointment we felt, I called this **Disappointment Island.**" It was renamed **Frémont Island,** out of respect of the lake's first scientific explorer, by Captain Howard Stansbury who made the first Government survey of Great Salt Lake in 1849-1850.

Frémont Pass (Iron) is the lowest altitude route across the range between the upper Sevier River valley and the Little Salt Lake valley; it is easier than the road down Red Creek Cañon—the way of the Spanish Trail. Frémont found this pass on August 2, 1853; Utah Highway 20 traverses it. **Frémont Pass** is *not* on Highway 91 near the Beaver-Iron line as some maps have it.

Frémont River, Dirty Devil River. On July 27, 1869, the Powell expedition came upon the mouth of a stream coming in from the right downstream from Cataract Cañon. One of the boats entered the stream; men from another boat inquired if it were a trout stream; the answer came: ". . . it is a 'dirty devil' "; "by this name the river is to be known hereafter. The water is exceedingly muddy, and has an unpleasant odor." "It slipped along between the low walls of smooth red sandstone to add its volume to the Colorado" (Powell). The name has since been changed to **Frémont River** (USBGN) in honor of Colonel John C. Frémont, the first scientific explorer of the Great Basin and the Far West.

Garfield is the site of Kennecott smelter and refinery on the narrow pass between the north end of the Oquirrh Mountains and the shore of Great Salt Lake; a community of the same name is nearby. A landing pier was built on the lake shore in the 1870's at which the steamboats *Kate Connor* and *City of Corinne* tied to load telegraph poles and railroad ties cut from the wooded Oquirrhs, and ores from the same range, to be transported across the lake destined for Corinne. The *City of Corinne* was later converted into a pretentious excursion steamboat which plied the lake between popular points. In the early autumn of 1880, during his campaign for the Presidency, General James A. **Garfield** enjoyed a lake excursion on this pleasure boat; afterward, the famous steamboat was renamed *General Garfield,* and the pier and resort were named **Garfield.** The boat, pier, and resort were destroyed by fire in 1904.

Garfield County, organized in 1882—being carved from eastern Iron County—extends from the crest of the Markagunt Plateau on the west to the Colorado River on the east with its north and south boundaries parallel. It was named in honor of James A. **Garfield** then recently assassinated President of the U.S.

Garrison (Millard) is a ranch hamlet in southern Snake Valley about one mile east of the Utah-Nevada boundary; the community is on **Snake Creek** and was first known by that name. It was a station on an old road from Salt Marsh in the north end of the valley, via Milford, to Pioche Nevada. A Mrs. **Garrison,** the village school teacher, cared for the mail and by association the hamlet adopted her name.

Geneva (Utah) was the name of a fruit-growing community on the northeast shorelands of Lake Utah; it was named from the city of **Geneva,** on the shore of Lac Léman, Switzerland. During War II the Government acquired the area and built an immense steel plant there—it being a convergent point for iron ore and coke transportation. After the War, this property was transferred to U.S. Steel Corporation. **Geneva** now connotes huge blast furnaces.

Gilbert Peak (Summit), 13,422 feet, is north of King's Peak in the central Uintas. It was named for Grove K. Gilbert, one of the original members of the USGS, who in 1874 gave the name "Lake Bonneville" to the Ice Age body of fresh water which covered much of the west-half of Utah.

Glen Cañon of the Colorado River extends downstream from the mouth of White Cañon to the mouth of Pah Reah Cañon, Arizona. Powell consolidated two previously named cañons: ". . . they now stand as **Glen Cañon** surrounded by red homogenous sandstone. It opened into many 'glens or coves' and we decided to call it **Glen Cañon.**" The word *glen* is of Celtic origin, meaning "narrow valley."

Glen Cañon Dam is thirteen miles downstream from the Utah-Arizona boundary. It is a unit of the Upper Colorado River Basin storage project. The impounded waters will drown the Colorado channel for 186 miles upstream; the reservoir will extend up the San Juan cañon seventy-one miles. Functions of this project are the control of the Colorado River and generation of hydroelectric power.

Goosenecks of the San Juan River are a series of closely set entrenched meanders, or oxbows, mostly west of Mexican Hat. From points of vantage a half-dozen of the oxbows are visible at once; they are a most striking example of stream erosion in an arid, flat country. The **Goosenecks** are photogenic.

Gosiute (Juab) is an Indian Reservation, west of the high Deep Creek Range, in northwestern Juab and extending into Nevada. **Goshute,** current variant, is a native village on the Reservation. **Gosiute** is the name of a Great Basin tribe concerning which there has been confusion as to their affiliations. The *Gosiute* are predominantly Shoshoni, linguistically wholly so. The etymology of the word is: *Gosi*, the prefix, is rooted in the Shoshoni *gosip* for "dust," referring to the dust storms of the salt desert; the suffix *ute* refers to the people. Their habitat was the most severe of the entire Shoshonean area; their poverty was pathetic; they lived in small valleys or at watering holes on the margin of the Great Salt Lake Desert.

Gothic Wash and **Mesa** (San Juan) are south of Río San Juan, southwest of Bluff. The name derives from the type of erosion dissection of the topography there—pointed arches—suggestive of Gothic architecture.

Goulding Trading Post (San Juan) is in Monument Valley just north of the Utah-Arizona boundary. The name is that of the founder and proprieter, Harry Goulding, who was one of the first licensed traders to the Navajo people. For decades white travelers have found **Goulding's** a haven of succor in the primitive Navajo Country.

Grand County is a large domain extending southward from Uintah County to San Juan, and eastward from the Green River to the Colorado State line. **Grand County** was organized in 1890; it derived its name from the **Grand River,** since 1921 the Colorado River, which runs diagonally from the Colorado line through the southeast area of the County, thence through the corner of San Juan to join the Green River to form the original Colorado River. The **Grand River** apparently derived its name from the preceding Spanish form *Río Grande del Norte;* it has its source high on the western slope of the Rocky Mountains.

Gray Cañon of the Green River is below Desolation Cañon; it extends from the Roan Cliffs to the mouth of Río San Rafael. **Gray** has a depth of 2,700 feet; it was thus named from the coloring of its walls by Powell in 1869.

Great Basin is the name first applied by Captain John C. Frémont to the area extending from the Wasatch Mountains on the east to the Sierra Nevada on the west; a region characterized by inland drainage, aridity of climate, and comparatively scanty flora and fauna. Frémont chose the adjective "great" to describe the extent, one-sixth of the area of the United States, and topographical importance of the **Great Basin.** Sovereignty of the **Great Basin** together with the remainder of *Nuevo Mexico* and *Alta California* passed from Mexico to the United States February 2, 1848.

Great Salt Lake was discovered by James Bridger late in 1824. He floated down the Bear River from the trappers' rendezvous in Cache Valley in a bullboat to decide a wager relative to the place where the Bear debouches. Bridger tasted of its water and reported his discovery of the salt water. It was then surmised that the salt water he discovered was an arm of the Pacific.

In the spring of 1826 four of William Sublette's men, based on the Rocky Mountain Fur Company's rendezvous at the site of Ogden, circumnavigated the Great Salt Lake in bullboats to determine any outlet and to make searching quests for new beaver streams. As a result of this exploration, the myth concerning the connection of Bridger's "salt water" with the Pacific Ocean was dispelled.

Captain B. L. E. Bonneville, who had never seen the great salt sheet, account of whose travels were glamorized and published by Washington Irving in 1836, had the audacity to give Bridger's "salt water" his own name on revised maps: Lake Bonneville. Bonneville's name did not adhere to the salt water. However, Bonneville was recompensed, posthumously, later in the century for this loss of wanted fame (*vide Lake Bonneville*).

John C. Frémont came north from *Río Severo* into Utah Valley on May 24, 1844, and encamped on the bottoms of Spanish Fork. Speaking of the Indian name of the principal affluent of Lake Utah, *Timpanogo* (Provo River), Frémont wrote: "It is probable that this river furnished the name which on the older maps has been generally applied to the **Great Salt Lake**; but for this I have preferred a name which will be regarded as highly characteristic . . ." The distinctive qualities of the waters of this lake required and received a name truly descriptive; and it was Captain John Charles Frémont who put the seal on the name on the maps: **Great Salt Lake.**

Great Salt Lake City, Salt Lake City, nineteen miles east of the lake shore, was founded by the Mormons on July 24, 1847, borrowing the name from that of the unique lake. A conference of the Mormon Church on August 7, 1847, resolved "that the city should be called Great Salt Lake City; that the creek should be called City Creek; and that the Utah Outlet (from Lake Utah) should be called the Western Jordan."

By extension, the name was applied to **Great Salt Lake County,** one of the original eight counties of the Territory of Utah, on September 9, 1850. The first descriptive word in the name of both city and county, for obvious practical reasons, was deleted January 29, 1868.

Great Salt Lake Desert is an area of low altitude extending westward and southwestward of Great Salt Lake and larger than it. The Salt Desert is hemmed in on the west by the Pilot Range north of Wendover and by the high Deep Creek Range to the southwest; on the east, by the Lakeside and Cedar Mountains in central Tooele County. This extensive Salt Desert was an extension of Great Salt Lake in recent geologic eras—both remnants of the Ice Age Lake Bonneville. The residual water was shallower but somewhat similar in salt content to the present lake, and as it was completely evaporated, a thick bed of salts remained. By extension, the **Desert** was named from that of the **Lake.** The Southern Pacific Railroad from the end of its causeway at Lakeside—the lowest point on the Salt Desert—traverses the desert to Lucin in the Pilot Range. The Western Pacific and Highway 40, after crossing Cedar Mountains, are parallel across the **Great Salt Lake Desert** to Wendover.

Green River, Río Buenaventura, Río Verde, has its source in the high Wind River Mountains in southwestern Wyoming; this drainage was Crow Indian territory and their name for the river was *Seeds-ke-dee Agee,* for "Prairie Hen River"; *Agee* is Crow for "river." By this name the upper reaches of the river were known in earliest exploratory times. The Shoshoni and Utes named the river *Ka'na,* their equivalent to Bitterroot, from the great abundance in its valley of this pink-flowered herb which gave them a favorite, nutritious tuber.

Green River runs southerly into Utah, where it is soon diverted easterly by the Uinta Mountains, coursing in that direction to flank the east shoulder of the Uintas and to form a grand loop in Colorado; thence southwesterly into the picturesque Cañon Lodore and Dinosaur National Monument to return into Utah; then, after veering almost to due south for long distances, makes a confluence with the Colorado River at the foot of Orange Cliffs in San Juan County.

In 1776 occurred a most remarkable, though objectively futile, *entrada* of Spanish explorers into the upper Colorado and Green River drainage areas and into the Great Basin. The urge for communication and consolidation between the two Spanish provinces of *Nuevo Mexico* and *Alta California* was stimulated by the Russian advance down the Pacific coast. The Dominguez-Escalante expedition was undertaken accordingly. The expedition set out to find an overland route from the upper Río Grande del Norte to Monterey via Lake Utah, although the existence and position of that lake was then hazy! A decade before, Don Juan Maria de Rivera had explored as far north as the present Gunnison River, and the country became well known to the Spanish; Spanish names were given the prominent natural features, most of which are still on the land. The Escalante party pursued a course generally northward from this area. They got into the Cliff Creek drainage which led them down to the Green River bottoms which they followed up to near the mouth of Split Mountain Cañon, above the site of Jensen, Utah. Here they forded the Green and named it *Río San Buenaventura; Buenaventura* is comprised of two words: *buena ventura,* "good fortune." *Padres Dominguez y Escalante* were the first Europeans on this mountain river; they pursued a westward course into the Great Basin and to Lake Utah. Other explorers, traders, and trappers from the upper Río Grande came into this region in the first half of the next century.

Green River was known to Americans in the trapper era—1820-1839—as the **Spanish River,** since there were Spanish explorers and traders along its course and because it was in Spanish then Mexico domain. These Spaniards gave the river a descriptive name: *Río Verde,* signifying "green river." Frémont has this reflection on Green River: "The refreshing appearance of the broad river, with its timbered shores and green-wooded islands, in contrast to its dry sandy plains, probably obtained for it the name Green River (*Río Verde*), which was bestowed by the Spaniards, who first came into this country about 1818." While on the Oregon Trail near South Pass, he wrote: " . . . to avoid the mountains about the head of Green River—*Río Verde* of the Spaniards." Gannett writes "Green River was so called from the green shale through which it flows." Currently, aerial photos taken with colored film in Red Cañon evidence a distinct green tint in the river. From heights above the cañons the water appears green to the eye.

The Old Spanish Trail crossed the Green at an old Ute crossing south of Book Cliffs; this historic crossing was to be known after 1853 as Gunnison Crossing. To the Spaniards who trod this Trail into the Great Basin to trade and to those who threaded the longer Spanish Trail from Santa Fé to Pueblo de los Angeles in the first half of the nineteenth century, the River was *Río Verde.* Spanish names originally applied to physiographic features were not tolerated by the Americans who were aliens operating in Spanish-Mexican domain. The names were invariably mutated into Americanized versions; thus, *Río Verde* signifying "green river" was named **Green River.** But, instead of leaving the correct and obvious at that, the Americans sought and conveniently found, near or far-off, a man named *Green* "for whom the river was named," they and later history writers said. Specifically, one of General Ashley's men was named *Green,* "after whom Green River is *supposed* to have been named" (Dellenbaugh). The merging of history and folklore is here exemplified.

Green River (Emery) is an historic outpost town at the west end of the Gunnison Crossing of **Green River.** U.S. Highways 6-50 cross the River here; State 24 stretches southerly to Hanksville, and from there 95 leads to Hite in Glen Cañon. **Green River** is a port of embarcation for boat trips down the Green-Colorado, including Cataract Cañon, to Hite and Glen Cañon Dam; and for river trips downstream only to the confluence, thence up the Colorado to Moab.

Gunnison (San Pete), a town on San Pitch Creek near its junction with the Sevier River, named for Captain J. W. Gunnison, head of a railroad survey in 1853.

Gunnison Crossing of Green River (Grand-Emery) is toward the head of **Gunnison Valley,** the open, broad lowland through which the river flows south of its emergence from Tavaputs Plateaus and their southern scarp, the Roan Cliffs. **Gunnison Butte** is east of the river; on the west is **Beckwith Plateau.** The three names of **Gunnison** were applied in honor of Captain

J. W. Gunnison, U.S. Reconnaissance Survey along the 39th Parallel for a route for a Pacific railroad; the plateau was named for Lieut. Beckwith, second in command. The party crossed the Green River here in 1853. Gunnison established the Latitude and Longitude and the altitude, 4,075 feet. This crossing of Green River has since borne his name.

From time immemorial, the Utes crossed the river here on rafts rudely constructed of logs bound with withes. The Americans William Wolfskill and George Yount were the first white men to cross here in the winter of 1830-31; they were on a long exploring and trapping trip from Taos, *Nuevo Mexico* to *Pueblo de los Angeles;* the route they explored became the main Spanish Trail—its beginning. There was no practicable crossing of the Green-Colorado between the Gunnison and the old Ute ford a long way downstream, *El Vado de los Padres,* and that was far more difficult of access as Fray de Escalante had experienced. Armijo crossed there, westward and eastward bound, to the *Mission de San Gabriel* in 1829-30. John C. Frémont crossed the Green here on his expedition of 1853-4. This strategic crossing of the Green River was bridged by the Denver and Río Grande Western Railroad in 1883; later, Highway 50 paralleled the rails.

Gunnison Massacre Monument (Millard): Southwest of Old Fort Deseret, toward the mouth of Sevier River, is the locale of the massacre of Captain J. W. Gunnison and seven of his men by Pah Vant Utes in 1853. A monument commemorates the disaster.

Harmony Creek (Washington) is the west originating branch of Ash Creek, arising northeast of Pine Valley Mountains; on its bank **Fort Harmony** was built and named in 1852 by John D. Lee; that was the southernmost white settlement. Later, a new hamlet was built, **New Harmony,** just west of present Highway 91. Lee's name implied agreement and concord between the settlers. This is a cluster-name.

Hat (Bird) Island is an islet in western Great Salt Lake, north of Carrington on the Stansbury peninsula axis. It was named from its cone-shape simulating a hat; its alternate name **Bird** refers to its having been a famous rookery. During the nesting season this islet was compactly covered with nests of gulls, pelicans, and cormorants. Great Salt Lake has greatly lowered in the last decade and this made it possible for predators to invade the rookery on **Bird**; in consequence, the birds have relocated their breeding grounds on Gunnison Island.

Heber, in the Upper Provo Valley, is the seat of Wasatch County. It is a dairy center. The town was named for **Heber** C. Kimball, a counselor to President Brigham Young; this was one Mormon mode of naming towns in pioneer times.

Helper (Carbon) was originally the name of a railroad station in Price Cañon about which a sizeable town has grown. The station was thus named because here the steep gradient westward onto the Wasatch Plateau necessitates attaching additional locomotives to trains —helpers.

Henry's Fork of Green River has its source in Henry's Fork Lake over the crest from King's Peak in the high Uintas; it flows northward into Wyoming, then eastward to come back into Utah and join the mother stream east of Linwood, Daggett County. **Henry's Fork** was named by General Ashley for his associate, Major Andrew **Henry,** in 1823. This is probably the oldest American place name in the Green River drainage.

Henry Mountains (Garfield) are a group of five discrete peaks ranging in altitude from 7,930 to 11,485 feet, west of the Frémont and Colorado Rivers. On the first Powell expedition in 1869 they were tentatively designated Unknown Mountains. On the Second Expedition of 1871-72, Dellenbaugh identified them as they went downstream: ". . . to the southwest rose the five beautiful peaks just beyond the mouth of the Dirty Devil." A. H. Thompson of this expedition headed an overland party to explore and study the geology of these mountains. They determined that lava from below had spread out between the sedimentary strata, forming what the party called 'blisters'; where one side of a 'blister' had been eroded, the surrounding stratifications were evident. Later, Grove K. Gilbert, USGS, after careful examinations, called these 'blisters' "laccolites (laccoliths), a mass of intrusive lava spreading between sedimentary beds and lifting the overlying strata into domes." The group was named **Henry Mountains** by Major John W. Powell in honor of the eminent Secretary of the Smithsonian Institution, Joseph **Henry,** under whose direction the explorations of the Colorado River domain were made by Powell. The discrete peaks were named by Powell for associates and **Mount Ellen,** the highest, for his sister, **Ellen** Powell Thompson.

Hiawatha (Carbon) is a coal-mining town southwest of Price at the east scarp of Wasatch Plateau. By extension, the town's name is that of the coal mine—the **Hiawatha.** In turn, the name of the mine was a transfer name from an important coal mine in Pennsylvania, and that name was for **Hiawatha,** the Mohawk chieftain who effected the League of the Iroquois, the Five Nations, and is also the name of the hero of Longfellow's **Hiawatha,** poem of an Iroquois legend.

High Plateaus of Utah is the name of the vast region south of Mount Nebo. Clarence E. Dutton, government geologist, in 1880 wrote a definitive geologic description in beautiful English of these uplifts: "The Wasatch as a distinct mountain range ends at Mount Nebo and it is here overlapped by a chain of plateau-uplifts which extend southward. These uplifts are distinguished by their tabular character." There are three ranges of High Plateaus: 1) West range is comprised of the Pah Vant at the north, the Tushar in the middle, and the Markagunt at the south; 2) the Sevier Valley separates the western from the middle range which consists of Sevier Plateau on the north and the Paunsaugunt on the south; and 3) Grass Valley and East Fork Sevier River are between the second and third ranges, which latter begins much farther north than the others: the lofty Wasatch Plateau overlapping the south end of the Wasatch Range, Fish Lake Plateau, Awapa, and the south member, which is the grandest of all, the Aquarius.

Hite (Garfield) is a Colorado River outpost near the mouth of Trachyte Creek. A ferry connects **Hite** with the mouth of White Cañon in San Juan County. This landing was named for Cass **Hite,** a placer gold prospector of the Colorado River cañons who found gold along the river and settled here in September, 1883. **Hite** is a port of embarcation for boats bound for Glen Cañon.

Hog Mountains (Box Elder) are off the northwest shore of Great Salt Lake. The name was applied by the Stansbury survey of 1849; it is a contraction of the generic descriptive term *hogback* referring to the contour of a hill or ridge formed by outcrops of vertical strata.

Holladay (Salt Lake) is an extensive suburban area southeasterly from Salt Lake City. The district was named in 1911 for John **Holladay,** an early settler on Big Cottonwood Creek which runs diagonally through the district.

Hooper (Weber), a village near the east shore of Great Salt Lake directly east of Frémont Island, was named for William H. Hooper, a Territorial Congressional Delegate.

Horseshoe Cañon (Daggett) of the Green River is just south of the Wyoming line; Flaming Gorge joins on the north. The river describes a horseshoe bow extending southeastward which suggested its name to Major Powell. Dellenbaugh describes the sequence of the first cañons of the Green thus: "Flaming Gorge is the gateway, **Horseshoe** the vestibule, and Kingfisher the ante-chamber of the whole grand series."

Hoskinnini Mesa (San Juan) is east of Navajo Mountain; this tableland was named for a Navajo headman. This is a hybrid name: the elements are from Navajo and Spanish, then absorbed into English.

Hovenweep National Monument (San Juan) is east of Montezuma Creek and north of Río San Juan. **Hoven-**

weep is comprised of four groups of prehistoric cliff dwellings, towers, and pueblos. Hackberry Cañon and Keely Cañon Groups are in Colorado; Ruin Cañon Cluster and Cajon Cañon Group are in Utah. The archaeology of these prehistoric ruins discloses various strata of ancient cultures: from the "Late Basket Maker" through the magnificent "Cliff Dweller" to the more recent eras characterized by the "Mesa-type Pueblo." The name **Hovenweep** is from the Ute tongue meaning "deserted valley"—a name most appropriate.

Huntsville (Weber) is a farming village in the upper Ogden River Valley—Ogden's Hole in the trapper era, where the *voyageurs,* trappers, and Indian associates held their rendezvous. The Mormon village was named to honor Captain Jefferson Hunt of the Mormon Battalion in the Mexican War.

Hurricane Hill (Washington) was the original application of the name **Hurricane;** afterwards, it was extended into a cluster of four distinct applications. The name was applied to a hill near a gulch, one of the few passes up the Hurricane Ledge, by a party of Mormon pioneers headed by Erastus Snow who were exploring for a road route, when they were overtaken by a severe storm. The word *hurricane* is derived ultimately from Spanish *huracán,* originally a cyclone, now a gale of unusual violence.

Hurricane Ledge, Cliffs, is a long prominent terrace or cliff 800 to 1000 feet high, extending in an almost unbroken line from Río Virgen southward to Grand Cañon. The Cliff is the western escarpment of Hurricane Bench and Little Creek Mountain in Utah and of the Uinkaret Plataeu in Arizona. The Second Powell Expedition, 1871-72, followed this long line of cliffs from the Uinkaret northward, the trip being recorded by Dellenbaugh: ". . . from this (**Hurricane Hill**) we applied the name **Hurricane Ledge** to the long line of sharp cliffs we had followed." In this particular terrain as here applied, the terms ledge and cliff are synonymous —southern segment of a long fault plane.

Hurricane (Washington), second largest town in this county, was settled in 1906. It is located on the south side of Río Virgen, across from La Verkin, at the west base of Hurricane Ledge or Terrace. The town was named from that of Hurricane Ledge, which physiographic feature was named nearly one-half century earlier. **Hurricane** is the center of a productive fruit-growing and turkey-raising district, the existence of which is the fruit of a canal eight miles long carved largely from solid rock at the turn of the century to convey Virgin River water onto productive land.

Hurricane Fault (Iron-Washington) is one of the longest and most conspicuous fault planes in America. Of this fault Dr. H. E. Gregory writes: "In the western part of the Colorado plateau province the master tetonic feature is the **Hurricane Fault**—a zone of fracture about 200 miles long within which the displacement of the sedimentary beds range from 1,500 to as much as 8,000 feet. In the topography the effects of the displacement are expressed by the Hurricane Cliffs that sharply define the western boundary of the Uinkaret and Markagunt plateaus and the intervening Hurricane and Kolob Terraces. The fault was first mapped and described by Dutton." Hurricane Cliffs mark the west escarpment of the upthrown mountain blocks of the fault. These cliffs are at their maximum near Cedar City where the fault upthrow now presents the magnificent mountains facing the valley. The downthrow is buried under great depths of detritus and alluvium forming the valley floor.

Ibapah, *Ai-bim-pah* (Tooele), in Deep Creek Valley north of Gosiute Reservation, was an Indian village site, later a ranch hamlet. *Ai-bim-pa* is the original Gosiute form of the word; Chamberlin gives this etymology: *ai-bi* for "clay", *m* an adjectival ending, and *pa* for "water." The water there is tinged with clay silt, his informant thus explained the origin of the aboriginal name. *Ibapah* is the Americanized version.

Ibex (Millard) is an old ranch. **Ibex** is the Latin species name of the Old World Alpine wild goat. The Basin ranges of western Utah and eastern Nevada were habitats of the indigenous Rocky Mountain goat, *Oreamnos montanus.* The name was applied to the locale because of the presence of wild goats. *Ibex* was also applied erroneously to the mountain sheep, *Ovis canadensis.* This was Gosiute (Shoshoni) territory and their name of the wild goat was *ka'-ni-runts.* Both species are conventionalized on petroglyphs in the region.

Indianola is a hamlet in northern San Pete County; it was an Indian village site. To the root word *Indian,* the locative case ending *ola* is appended, indicating a place.

Indian Springs (Tooele) is an oasis in the southern end of Skull Valley; it has been a Gosiute watering hole and village site from time unknown.

Iosepa (Tooele) is a ranch in central Skull Valley. This name is not Gosiute, though the terminal *pa* could easily mislead as the familiar Shoshoni suffix for "water." *Iosepa* is a modified Hawaiian version of the Christian name Joseph. Late in the nineteenth century the Mormon Church sponsored the immigration of a group of Hawaiians and attempted to settle the colony in Skull Valley. The site was named for Joseph F. Smith who was a missionary in Hawaii; later, he was president of the Church. The settlement was a failure.

Iron City (Iron) is a ghost town—the site of the ruins of an ambitious pioneer industry, the second attempt to smelt iron ores at their source. **Iron City** is on the banks of Little Pinto near the south base of Iron Mountain, 7,828 feet, a rich mass of magnetite and hematite ores in the Iron Range. The ruins comprise a well-preserved mammoth charcoal oven, blast furnace, primitive stone-lined pit for grinding the ores, and a pretentious residence. Since coking coal had not been found for smelting the iron ore, large quantities of timber were reduced to charcoal in beehive-shaped ovens. Lack of coking coal and with the railroad bringing iron products from the East after 1869, this pioneer attempt to smelt iron ores was abandoned. Three-fourths of a century later in the early 1940's, the ores from this same Iron Mountain and other deposits in the Iron Range were transported 250 miles to the great government-built blast furnaces at Geneva.

Iron County was one of the original eight in Utah Territory. Prior to the Act of Congress creating the Territory in 1850, the area now embraced in **Iron County** together with an almost boundless expanse across the Colorado Plateaus on the east and to the Sierra Nevada on the west, was known as "Little Salt Lake County," thus named from **Little Salt Lake** in the sink of the Parowan Valley. Reconnaisance of the region in 1849 disclosed iron ore in the Iron Range to the southwest; in consequence of this discovery, plans were made to colonize the Little Salt Lake Valley; and **Iron County** was established by decree as the first step for colonization. The County was thus named from the large bodies of ores within its bounds, on the west of Cedar Valley.

Iron County Mission was organized under the leadership of George A. Smith to colonize the new county and to attempt to smelt iron ore. This Mission, comprised of 119 men, 310 women, and 18 children, set forth from Great Salt Lake City, December 7, 1850, and arrived at the site of Parowan, January 13, 1851. Parowan was the first settlement south of Provo on the Mormon Trail.

Iron Springs (Iron) wells up at the head of a gap through the **Iron Range** which connects Cedar Valley on the east with the Escalante Desert on the west. North of the pass are Three Peaks; to the south, the well-known landforms of Swett Peak, Desert Mound, and further south, Iron Mountain, all iron-ore peaks.

Jensen (Uintah) is a village at the west end of the Green River crossing of Highway 40. A five-mile, terminal road leads northward from **Jensen** to the museum and quarry in Dinosaur National Monument. This crossing was named for Lars **Jensen** who settled here in

1877 and started a ferry service across the Green in 1885.

Jordan River (Utah-Salt Lake) drains surplus water from fresh-water Lake Utah into Great Salt Lake. It was first named from its originating lake—**Utah River;** then the name **Utah Outlet** was popularly applied to the stream until 1847. The Mormon pioneers, observing the striking similarity of Lake Utah-Great Salt Lake drainage to that of the Biblical Sea of Galilee with the Dead Sea, named the connecting stream **Western Jordan** by a resolution in conference on August 7, 1847. Later, the name was changed to **Jordan River** which name became firmly affixed.

Juab (Juab) is a railroad station in the south end of Juab Valley from which it was named. The Utah Southern Railway had successive termini at Lehi, *Juab,* and Frisco.

Juab County, created in 1852, is in west-central Utah extending from the Wasatch Range westward to the Nevada line. The eastern fourth of its boundary is very irregular, following the crests of several short mountain ranges; west of Tintic Mountains, **Juab's** north-south dimension is narrow in comparison with Tooele on the north and Millard County on the south. By extension, the county was named from that of Juab Valley.

Juab Valley, in the eastern part of the county, parallels the west base of Mount Nebo and continuing mountains; the main population, agriculture and industry are in this valley. *Yoab* was the earlier form of the name; this was used in the Third Epistle of the Mormon Presidency. Bancroft writes, *Yo-ab* is the name of a friendly Sampitches Ute; the word signifies "flat or level" and is in reference to the **Juab Valley floor.** In eastern Utah, the White River Utes called the plain at the confluence of the Duchesne, Green, and White rivers *Yu-av,* that is "flat or level."

Junction, the seat of Piute County, is a small village near the *junction* of Sevier River with its main tributary, East Fork, coming in from the east.

Kaiparowitz(s) (Kai-par′-o-witz) **Plateau,** 7,000 feet, is a long, narrow, irregularly dissected tableland in south-central Garfield County and extending southeasterly through Kane to the Colorado River. The west scarp of the latter segment is sharply scalloped; its east scarp, known as Straight Cliffs, is sheer—from 7,000 down to 5,000 feet, then gradually to 4,000—the floor of the Escalante River Valley. The **Kaiparowitz** forms a southeastern backdrop, across the Pahreh Valley, for Bryce Amphitheatre. **Kaiparowitz Peak,** 9,180 feet, surmounts the plateau east of Henrieville.

Kaiparowitz(s) was "the Pah Ute name for a small elevation near the north end," likely **Kaiparowitz Peak,** and the name was extended to the whole irregular elevation by A. H. Thompson of the Second Powell Expedition in 1871-72. **Kaiparowitz** was also the name of the Pah Ute group which occupied the region. The etymology of the word is: *Kaip* is a variant of *kaib,* "mountain"; *aro* is a possessive element; the suffix *witz* is a widely used Pah Ute word for "family or people"; that is, "the mountain home of these people."

Kamas (Summit) is a town on Beaver Creek, one of the originating branches of Weber River, in Rhodes Valley, at the west base of the Uinta Mountains. The name is an extension of **Kamas Prairie** on which the town is located.

Kamas Prairie (Summit) was in aboriginal times an extensive, rolling grassland along Beaver Creek and the upper Rhodes Valley. On the meadow grew a species of plant, *Camassia quamash,* of the lily family with blue flower and succulunt bulb resembling the hyacinth. The words *kamash, kamas* were early forms of *camas* which came into English from the Chinook jargon (Northwest) signifying "sweet". The bulbs of the *kamas* were a staple food of the Indians, prepared by steaming in heated pits, and deposited in caches for winter provisions. In aboriginal times the *kamas* grew luxuriantly on the headwaters of the Weber and for this reason the name was given this meadow land. Frémont, while going down the Bear River Valley below Soda Springs on August 26, 1843, wrote: "We obtained from them (Shoshoni) a small quantity of roots of different kinds in exchange for goods. Among them was a sweet root of very pleasant flavor, having somewhat the taste of preserved quince. Among the Indians lower down on the Columbia it is the celebrated *kamas, Camassia esculenta.*"

Kamas Prairie was the rendezvous of General Ashley, who had navigated down the Green River from Henry's Fork in 1823 and came overland up the Du Chesne River, and the mountaineers who had been in Utah valleys the year previous: Provot, J. S. Smith, Sublette, Bridger, and Jackson.

Kanab (Kane), a ranch town, was located on the bank of Kanab Creek and given its name, an old pattern in name choosing. **Kanab** is the county seat; it has become a thriving, strategic tourist center, being the gateway to the famous Kaibab Plateau and Forest and North Rim of Grand Cañon, to Navajo Bridge and the Painted Desert, and on new Highway 89 to the Glen Cañon Bridge and Dam—all in Arizona.

Kanab Creek (Kane) flows south from the south rim of the Great Basin to cross the Arizona line and continue in a deep, narrow cañon into Grand Cañon and the Colorado. The word *kanab* is Pah Ute for "willow"; the name was given the creek by the Indians because of a lush growth of willows along its upper reaches. *Kanab* has been naturalized into English.

Kanarraville (Iron) is at the west base of Kolob Terrace. Traversing the narrow valley opposite the village, is an imperceptible crest forming here the south rim of the Great Basin. The word *Kanarra* derives from the name of a Pah Ute headman, *Quanarrah,* whose permanent camp was worsted by the Mormon village; the suffix *ville* denotes village; this is a hybrid name, the two elements coming from different languages.

Kane County is central of the tier of three southern counties. Most of its area is south of the plateau country and is of comparatively low altitude; nearly all is in the Colorado River drainage. **Kane County** was named in honor of Colonel Thomas L. Kane of Philadelphia, a sincere friend of the Mormon people, and through whose prestige in Washington the stress of the "Mormon War" was relieved. An heroic bronze statue of Colonel Kane was placed in the rotunda of Utah State Capitol in 1959.

Kanosh (Millard) is an agricultural village on Kanosh Creek at the foot of Pah Vant Plateau fifteen miles south of Fillmore. The name of creek and town is for a famous Pah Vant headman, *Kan-osh.* This Ute word *kan-osh* seems to have meant "man of white hair." Between the town and the base of the plateau is the small **Kanosh Indian Reservation,** set aside as the home of the remnant of the Pah Vant Utes. Steward writes that necessary transactions with the whites, who, after 1847, pre-empted Indian village sites and food areas along the Wasatch and Plateau piedmonts, rapidly elevated chiefs to prominent positions. The Pah Vants were represented by *Kan-osh* who won some concessions for them.

Kanosh Creek and **Kanosh** were called by the early whites **Corn Creek** because the Indians were raising maize here when the first Caucasians came into the Pah Vant Valley. This stream marked about the northern extremity of the area of aboriginal horticulture. Archaeology has disclosed that on the banks of **Kanosh Creek** lived a prehistoric people possessing a modified Basket Maker culture; they built of adobe pueblo-type, rectangular, one-story, communal buildings; they practiced horticulture intensively.

Kennecott Copper Corporation, Utah Division, owns the world's greatest open-pit, low-grade, copper mine in Bingham Cañon. The Corporation was named indirectly for Dr. Robert **Kennicott,** an explorer and developer of Alaska a century ago. A mining district in Alaska was named for him. A mine in this district was developed by *Kennecott* Mines Company—the original operation of the present great enterprise. The *i* in the surname was corrupted to *e* in the company's name.

Kingfisher Cañon (Daggett) is downstream from Horseshoe of Green River. "The air was full of kingfishers darting about and we immediately called the creek, a small tributary, by their name." "The name *Kingfisher* we gave the gorge for the same reason we had called the creek at our camp by that name; these birds were numerous" (Dellenbaugh)

King's Peak (Duchesne), 13,498 feet, is the highest point in Utah; it is on the crest of the central High Uintas. **King's Peak** was named for Clarence *King,* geologist, one of the original members and first head of the United States Geological Survey in 1879.

Kolob Cañons are south and west of Kolob Terrace: La Verkin Creek drains the area. To the northwest corner of Zion National Park, an area embracing **Kolob Cañons** was annexed in 1957. Strangely, these cañons have not been fully explored. They are very narrow and almost as deep as Zion; the walls are sheer cliffs of varied red sandstone for the greater area; the intervening ridges are sharp and narrow with scanty vegetation; **Kolob Cañons** are of spectacular scenic interest. The Hurricane Fault Cliffs form the western scarp of the area, and along their base Highway 91 traverses. Superb views of the high, sheer, red cliffs split with narrow crevasses are obtained by driving westward across the narrow valley to New Harmony. The name of the cañons is an extension of that of the terrace.

Kolob Terrace, 8,000-9,000 feet. In delineating the area and describing its geology, Dr. Herbert Gregory wrote: "Essentially the Kolob Terrace is a bench cut into the face of the ancient Markagunt Plateau." It extends from Coal Creek southward, and is drained partially into the Great Basin, the southern part into Río Virgen. "The surface of the Kolob is characterized by rounded hills that slope gently downward to broad valley floors. Every part of the surface is covered by organized drainage and many square miles are so thickly mantled with soil that rock outcrops are rare." The name **Kolob** is not of Indian origin; it is the name of the major star in Mormon cosmography—a postulated center of the universe. The application of the name **Kolob** to the **Terrace** is undetermined.

Koosharem, 6,800 feet, is a village near the southern boundary of Sevier County, in Grass Valley through which Otter Creek flows southward. This is an old Indian village site. **Koosharem Reservation** extends southward into Piute. Before Caucasian displacement, there was a group of Utes occupying this area and up the Sevier Valley known as Pavagowunsin. After the Ute alliance, the Government settled remnants of these Ute bands with some intermixture of Pah Ute from farther south on the reservation. Fish Lake, in the mountains to the east, was an important aboriginal food source favorable to concentration of Indian population here. The word *koosharem* referred to an edible tuber which was a food staple of these Utes.

Labyrinth Cañon of the Green River extends downstream from the San Rafael Valley to the confluence with the Colorado; it was so named by Major Powell because of the exceeding tortuosity of the river's course in this region; many of the entrenched meanders or oxbows are astounding; the walls are sheer, deep red, and of arresting grandeur. **Labyrinth Cañon** exemplifies the terrific power of stream erosion on a level terrain in an arid climate. Powell wrote: "It grows deeper with every mile of travel; the walls are symmetrically curved, grandly arched, of a beautiful color which is reflected in the quiet waters, so as to almost deceive the eye and suggest the thought that the beholder is looking into profound depths. We name the expanse **Labyrinth Cañon.**"

Laguna is a place on the shore of Lake Utah. The word is Spanish for "lake" or "lagoon"; the name harks back to the Dominguez-Escalante expedition of 1776. Fray Dominguez called the people whose villages were on the eastern shores **Lagunas,** i.e., "lake people."

Lake Bonneville[1] was the name given by the eminent

[1]Rufus Wood Leigh, "Bonneville: The Lake Name," *Utah Historical Quarterly,* April, 1958.

geologist Grove Karl Gilbert in 1875 to the extinct Ice Age body of fresh water which covered a large area in the eastern part of the Great Basin: "**Lake Bonneville**—From considerations . . . I have come to regard as phenomena of the Glacial epoch a series of lakes, of which the beaches and sediments are to be found at many points in the Great Basin. The greatest of these . . . covered a large area in western Utah, including the valleys now occupied by Sevier, Utah, and Great Salt Lake, and its limits and history have been so far indicated by our examinations, *that I venture to propose for it the name Bonneville,* in honor of Captain B. L. E. Bonneville . . ." This Pleistocene lake continues to elicit much geologic study.

Captain Bonneville, U.S. Army, while on leave of absence, explored and exploited the fur trade in the basins of the Bear, Snake, and Columbia rivers, 1832-34; he was never in the Salt Lake Valley. Account of his travels were glamorized and published by Washington Irving in 1837.

Lake Navajo (Kane), a small, interesting mountain tarn, lies almost hidden in narrow Duck Creek Valley near the south margin of the Markagunt Plateau. G. K. Gilbert, USGS, in the first geological exploration and study of the Markagunt, noted that "Mountain Lakelet (Lake Navajo) lies in a valley of erosion, between limestone walls, and is retained by fresh lava streams which have filled the lower portion of the eroded valley." The waters of this picturesque lake have a subterranean outlet through the lava and underlying Wasatch formation into the drainage of North Fork Virgin River, issuing in Cascade Springs—over the southern ridge. **Navajo Lake** was so named because the Navajo, whose homelands are across the Colorado River to the southeast, came into this area to raid the Pah Ute, and later to make raids for horses and sheep from the whites. *Mountain Lakelet* (Gilbert) was renamed to commemorate a skirmish near the lake between Navajo raiders and stockmen from Cedar City.

"The Pah Ute name of this lake is *Pah-cu-ay,* meaning 'Cloud Lake'" (Palmer).

Lake Powell is the specific name the Department of the Interior has given Glen Cañon Reservoir to honor the memory of Major John Wesley Powell, veteran of Shiloh, the original explorer of the Green-Colorado cañons from Green River, Wyoming, to Grand Wash, Arizona, in 1869, and who named Glen and all other cañons of the Green-Colorado system. The name is approved by USBGN. The impounded waters of **Lake Powell** will drown the Colorado channel for 186 miles upstream—to a point not far below the confluence of the Green and Colorado; the lake will also extend up the San Juan cañon for seventy-one miles. The bulk of the water will be confined within the sheer, massive Navajo sandstone walls of the main cañons. Functions of the reservoir are primarily the control of the Colorado River and the generation of hydroelectric power.

La Sal Mountains, Abajo Mountains to the south, Henry Mountains west of the Colorado, and lone Navajo Mountain south of the San Juan, are laccoliths—formed by eruptive forces which did not reach the surface. Intrusions of igneous material domed the overlying strata, and through subsequent erosion the igneous character was exposed. **La Sal National Forest** comprises not only **La Sal Mountains** but also Abajo Mountains and Elk Ridge to the south.

Sierra de Sal are two clusters of high, rounded peaks, ranging in altitude from 12,004 to 12,721 feet, usually snow-clad, east of the Colorado River in Grand and San Juan Counties. *Sierra de Sal* bulked large as a distant headland on the Old Spanish Trail from Santa Fé. The name is Spanish: *Sierra,* "a serrated mountain range"; and *de sal,* "of salt"; *la sal,* "the salt." The Spanish so named these mountains from salt springs found near their base. Frémont noted: "Salt is abundant on the eastern border mountains, as the *Sierra de Sal* being named from it." The Americanized name *La Sal Mountains* is hybrid, elements of two languages.

La Sal is a ranch hamlet on the south base of the mountains from which it is named. The Spanish Trail came this way.

Las Vegas de Santa Clara (Washington) was near the head of Pinto Creek at the south rim of the Great Basin. From 1830 this was a favorite camping haven on the Spanish Trail; here the men and stock could rest and fortify against the sterile and hot deserts to the southwest. The etymology of *Las Vegas de Santa Clara* is: *Las* is the plural definite article; *Vegas,* plural, was widely used in Spanish America to signify "an open, fertile, marshy or grassy plain" in contrast to the sterile desert expanse. The name thus signified "The Meadows of Santa Clara." Frémont, traveling northward from California May 12, 1844, wrote: "Our animals were somewhat repaid for their hard marches by an excellent camping ground on the summit of the ridge, which forms here the dividing chain between the waters of Río Virgen and those flowing northwardly and belonging to the Great Basin (Pinto Creek) . . . we found here an extensive mountain meadow, rich in bunch grass, and fresh with numerous springs of clear water. It was those *Las Vegas de Santa Clara,* where the annual caravan from California to New Mexico halted and recruited for some weeks."

Mountain Meadows: After 1847, increasing numbers of Americans supplanted the Spanish on the Spanish Trail; *Las Vegas de Santa Clara* became known as the *Mountain Meadows;* and the Spanish Trail, the "Mormon Trail." It was on this camping and grazing haven in September, 1857, that a caravan of 140 immigrants from Missouri and Arkansas, California bound, possessing much livestock and stores, were butchered—the notorious Mountain Meadows Massacre.

La Verkin is an attractive fruit-growing village on the rich bottom lands above the confluence of La Verkin Creek with Río Virgen. It is noted for the lovely blossoms of its almond orchards in springtime and the choice almonds in autumn. Hard by are the *La Verkin*

Hot Springs, frequented hopefully by the halt and arthritic. **La Verkin** was settled in 1897 by the Thomas Judd family of St. George. The village name is an extension of that of the Creek.

La Verkin Creek (Washington) drains the southwestern part of Kolob Terrace and Kolob Cañons, then flows southerly parallel with Ash Creek which joins it just north of its confluence with Río Virgen. A high, narrow, lava-covered ridge intervenes between the two creeks. The name *La Verkin* was extant "when the first Americans began exploring the Río Virgen region" (*Deseret News,* April 3, 1852). This creek must have been named by Spanish explorers or traders from Santa Fé early in the 19th century, but the correct Spanish name was not absorbed into American toponymy; the name was badly corrupted. There is no reference to its origin or significance in historic literature. Corruption of Spanish and Indian names was almost the rule rather than the exception in early American times in this region. As the creek is a tributary of *Río de la Virgen,* and the name of a tributary sometimes follows the prototype name, it is most probable that *La Verkin* is a shortened and corrupted form of the name of the mother stream: *Río de la Virgen.* There is no *k* in Spanish; but the *k* sound in *Verkin* is quite similar to the Spanish *g* in *Virgen.*

Leeds (Washington) is a picturesque pioneer hamlet on Highway 91 southeast of Pine Valley Mountains which was settled by Mormon immigrants from Leeds, Yorkshire, England, who named the hamlet for their former home.

Leidy Peak (Uintah), 12,013 feet, is on the crest of the High Uintas; Ashley Creek has its source south of this peak. **Leidy Peak** was named to honor one of America's noted paleontologists, Joseph *Leidy* of Philadelphia. His researches resulted in several important monographs, one being *The Fossil Horse.*

Levan (Juab) is a farming village eleven miles south of Nephi; it was settled in 1868. **Levan** is at the fork of the highway: US 91 continues southwestward; Utah 28 leads south to the Sevier River Valley connecting with US 89. On **Levan** ridge, traversing the valley to the north, "dry-land farming," using seeds and methods adapted to light rainfall, was first developed in Utah. **Levan** is at the base of the mountains where the eastern horizon is lowest—where the sun rises in the southern part of the valley. The name derives from cropping the French word *levan*(*t*) which means "the east or point where the sun rises." *The Levant* has come to mean specifically lands that lie upon and stretch away from the eastern shores of the Mediterranean, "the lands of the sunrise."

Little Dolores River, Río Dolores Chiquito (Grand), heads west of Grand Junction, Colorado, having a short course across the Utah line to the Colorado River. This stream was named by the Spanish from the larger *Río Dolores* (*q.v.*) to the south; *Chiquito* is Spanish for "little."

Little Salt Lake (Iron) is a thin brackish sheet in the sink of Parowan Valley; Red Creek and Center Creek drain into it; **Parowan Lake** is the colloquial name. *Little Salt Lake* was named in contrast to Great Salt Lake in early exploratory times. My informant, Wootz Parashontz, gave the Pah Ute name as *Paragoon* which implies "vile water"; and this word is the root of the name of the village to its southeast, *Paragoonah;* also, the name *Parowan* has evolved from *Paragoons,* "marsh people", the name of the Pi-Ede band living near the *Paragoon.*

Loa (Wayne), a village in the narrow Frémont Valley, is the county seat. This is a transfer name made by a Mormon missionary to Hawaii: the name of one of two active volcanoes on the Island of Hawaii, Hawaii—*Mauna Loa,* meaning "long mountain." This transfer to the Frémont Valley seems incongruous.

Logan (Cache), the county seat and home of Utah State University, is Utah's fourth city in population, 18,731, and is a most attractive small city on the banks of Logan River at the mouth of Logan Cañon. **Logan** was named directly from *Logan River* which is a common mode of naming towns. The site was selected by Peter Maughn, who had settled Wellsville, in the spring of 1859.

Logan River (Cache) was named for **Logan** Fontanelle, a friendly Indian chief (Gannett). The name *Logan Fontanelle* was bestowed by French-Canadians on a Plains Chieftain of great personality and commanding influence. Logan River and Cache Valley were part of the domain of French-Canadian trappers in the era 1820-1839. Thus, a French name was bestowed upon a great Indian, then the name was transferred to a physiographic feature in a different region.

Lucin (Box Elder) is a Southern Pacific Railroad station on the western edge of the Great Salt Lake Desert at the foot of Pilot Range. The station was first named *Pilot Peak* from the historic peak in this range. The name *Lucin* derives from the generic element of the name of a suborder of bivalve fossils, *Lucina subanta,* which were exposed with the shrinkage of Lake Bonneville. **Lucin** was a station on the original Central Pacific Railroad which rounded the northern end of Great Salt Lake. After the turn of the century, the successor Southern Pacific greatly shortened the mileage and reduced grades and curves by building the *Lucin Cutoff* between **Lucin** and Ogden which entailed the construction of a wooden-trestle causeway across the lake. The old wooden structure has recently been supplanted with an expensive rock fill.

Lund (Iron) is the junction station on the Union Pacific Railroad for the Cedar City branch line. **Lund** was named, when the Los Angeles and Salt Lake Railroad was extended from Milford to California, for Robert C. **Lund** of St. George, a business man, director of the railroad, and friend of the builder of the new road, Senator W. A. Clark of Montana.

Lynndyl (Millard) is the railroad junction of the original road from Salt Lake City via Provo with the road built after the turn of the century via Tooele. When the latter road was being built, a lady telegrapher at the end-of-construction was asked from Salt Lake: "Where are you?" Being at an unnamed point, she was non-plused for a moment, then noticed the imprint on her shoe which she had just taken off because of tired feet —"Lynn, Mass.," and forthwith answered, "At Lynn." She thereby named the junction station. When designated for a post office, the Postal Service required a modification of the name as there was a post hamlet on the Raft River in northwestern Utah named *Lynn;* so the euphonious suffix *dyl* was appended. This is a true rail-lore story vouched by Joel L. Priest, Jr., Union Pacific Railroad.

Magotsu Creek (Washington) is a tributary of the Santa Clara. This name is Pah Ute. "It is a corruption of *Ma-haut-su* for 'long slope' " (Palmer).

Malad River (Box Elder) runs south from southern Idaho into Utah and has a confluence with the Bear River some ten miles north of Great Salt Lake. The word *malad* derives from the French adjective *malade* meaning "sick": *Que n'est pas en bonne santé.* This name was bestowed on the stream by trappers of Hudson's Bay Company in the 1820's. The trappers ate the flesh of the beavers inhabiting the valley which had lived on poison roots.

Mammoth Peak (Juab), 8,104 feet, is the highest peak in the Tintic Mining District. **Mammoth,** an old boom mining camp, is at the peak's west base. **Mammoth** is a descriptive adjective derived from the name of a very large extinct elephant, and means huge, very high, colossal. In the vernacular, it was a common hyperbole, in this instance implying a tremendously rich and large mine.

Manila is the seat of Daggett County; the town is just south of the Utah-Wyoming boundary and a short distance west of the mouth of Henry's Fork of Green River. The town's name was applied subsequent to the Spanish-American War in reference to Dewey's Naval victory in **Manila** Bay, Philippine Islands. There is a trend to transfer alien names after our foreign wars.

Manti (San Pete) is the county seat; it was founded in 1849 on a branch of San Pitch Creek. "The name Manti was suggested by Brigham, who declared that on this spot should be raised one of the cities spoken of in the *Book of Mormon,* and here he built with his own hands an adobe house" (Bancroft). On a commanding eminence overlooking city and valley is the LDS Manti Temple, a beautiful structure of cream-colored oolite.

Mantua Valley (Box Elder) is a small, roundish valley at the head of Box Elder Creek in the Wasatch Mountains east of Brigham City. The name is French, a heritage of the trapper era, 1820-1839, when French-Canadians in the employ of Hudson's Bay Company combed this region for the beaver. The word *mantua* appears to be a corruption of the name of a loose cloak in fashion in the first part of the 19th century—*manteau. Le manteau, habit que nous portens sur les autres.*

Markagunt Plateau (Iron-Garfield) is the south member of the west range of the High Plateaus which extend southward from Mount Nebo where the Wasatch Range terminates. "These uplifts are distinguished by their tabular character" (Dutton). The eastern, northern, and western parts of the **Markagunt** drain into the Great Basin, the southern areas are in the Colorado drainage. The **Markagunt** has a general elevation of 9,000 to 10,000 feet, and is surmounted by Brian Head, 11,315 feet, Hancock Peak, 10,500 feet, and other high mountains "The surface of the Markagunt Plateau, developed on sedimentary rock and lava, is characterized by gentle slopes, slow-running streams" (Gregory). At the east of the headland, Mammoth Creek, a choice trout stream, flows eastward—an originating branch of Sevier River. Hancock Peak, Houston Mountain, and neighboring volcanic cones retain their summit craters, and from their sides extend streams of lava marked by features of recent flows. Forests of many species of conifers and quaking aspen, interspersed by mountain parks, open meadow lands, cover the high terrain. The comparatively flat areas furnish summer grazing for herds of sheep. Mule deer and cougar abound. The name **Markagunt** is of Pah Ute origin, meaning "highland of trees," and was applied by A. H. Thompson, close associate of Major J. W. Powell.

Marysvale is a picturesque channel or narrow valley of Sevier River in northern Piute County. The vale lies at the east base of the Tushar Plateau. This front of the Tushar is arrestingly lofty and sheer and is gashed by rugged cañons. The walls of the vale in places are variegated conglomerate formations which are mineralized with precious and rare elements. The Spanish Trail, following up *Río Severo,* threaded this defile, and it is most likely that it was named for the Virgin Mary early in the nineteenth century.

Marysvale is a village which nestles in the vale; it has been a mining center for gold, silver, uranium, alunite, and other rare metals. Big Rock Candy Mountain, north of the village, is a tourist attraction; nearby are rock and mineral collections, and there is a small zoo of recently captured fauna of the region. The village was named by extension from the vale.

Mexican Hat (San Juan), deep in the Goosenecks of Río San Juan, is the site of an old ferry crossing, more recently a bridge, and is a strategic outpost for travelers entering the Navajo Country from the north. A mill for processing uranium ores has been built here. The name is in reference to an eroded monolithic column rising some 200 feet above the valley floor which is surmounted by a more resistant capstone measuring sixty feet in diameter and twelve feet thick; this top rock simulates in outline the well-known Mexican sombréro.

Midway (Wasatch) is a village on the west side of the Upper Provo Valley; it is noted for its hot calcareous springs, colloquially called "hot pots," which have built up several tufa cones. The village site was chosen *midway* between two earlier farming areas, hence the name *Midway.*

Milford (Beaver) is an historic town on the Union Pacific Railroad in the northern course of the Beaver River valley. For many years **Milford** was near the terminus of the railroad—to the west at Frisco—and from it freight was forwarded to several southern Utah counties and to eastern Nevada. Passengers traveled long distances to entrain. In 1904 the rails were extended southwesterly to southern California. **Milford** was so named from the following circumstance. An ore-reduction mill stood on the hill west of the river; four-horse teams hauling ore-laden wagons from the Mineral Range on the east side of the valley had to ford the river to reach the mill. Combining the two words *mill* and *ford,* thus related, the town founders coined the name **Milford.**

Millard County and its seat, **Fillmore,** were named for President **Millard Fillmore.** President Fillmore signed the Act creating the Territory of Utah, September 9, 1850, and appointed Brigham Young first Governor. **Millard** is one of Utah's largest counties, extending from the crest of the Pah Vant Plateau and its northern extensions on the east, to the Nevada line on the west; and its north-south dimension is nearly seventy miles.

Mirror Lake (Duchesne) is just south of the northwest crest of the Uinta Mountains; it nestles sky-high in a cluster of 12,000-foot peaks; and is the source of North Fork Duchesne River. Within a short radius three other rivers have their source: to the southwest flows the Provo; to the west the Weber; and to the north the Bear River begins its circuitous course. A good Forest Service highway leads from Kamas—Utah 150—and this Service has provided a recreational area at which your image in **Mirror Lake** is attained.

Moab, the seat of Grand County, is in the southern part of the county south and east of the Colorado River in the mouth of Spanish Valley; it is on US 160. **Moab** was settled in 1876. Presently it is the hub of uranium mining and milling on the Colorado Plateaus. **Moab** was named from the Kingdom of *Moab,* lying east of the Jordan and Dead Sea, the land of the Semetic Moabites, a people who revolted against the King of Israel: II Kings, 3.

Modena (Iron) is a Union Pacific station at the southwest margin of Escalante Desert, just east of the Nevada line. **Modena** is the name of a city, an art center, in Emilia, northern Italy. The station could have been named for the Italian city; the railroad has no record of the origin of station names in this section. The root of *modena* is *mode,* signifying "the current manner of being or doing."

Mona (Juab) is a farming village at the base of Mount Nebo in the northern end of Juab Valley; it was founded in 1852. The origin of the name is undetermined. **Mona** is the ancient name of Anglesey, Anglesea, an island and county in Wales. The town may have been founded by Welsh immigrants. Or, the name could be the first word of the name of Leonardo da Vinci's famous portrait the "Mona Lisa" done about 1500, here the meaning is "Madam Lisa." **Mona** is a common feminine given name.

Monte de Crísto, Monte Crísto Peak (Rich), 9,138 feet, is a conspicuous landform on the east shoulder of the Wasatch Mountains on the divide between the Ogden and Bear River drainages. This area was the domain of both French-Canadian and American beaver trappers during the era 1820-1839. The French name should have appeared on the maps. The first name above is Italian, literally, "Mountain of Christ"; the second form is hybrid, corrupted, and repetitive.

Montezuma Creek is a northern tributary of the San Juan heading in the vicinity of Monticello. The San Juan Mission made a settlement at the mouth of this creek in 1880. The name **Montezuma** is an American variant of the name of the last Aztec Emperor of Mexico, Moctezuma II, who was killed by Cortez in 1520. The names **Montezuma** and **Aztec** have been promiscuously applied to various ancient pueblos and cliff dwellings in the Southwest because they were supposed to have been once occupied by the Aztecs. Hodge declares there is no ground in fact for the belief that any Southwest pueblo or other habitation is of Mexican origin. Eastward from **Montezuma Creek** the country is rich in prehistoric communal dwellings (*vide* Hovenweep).

Montezuma Peak (Tooele), 7,369 feet, in the Deep Creek Range southwest of the Great Salt Lake, is in Gosiute territory. There must have been some evidence of ancient Indian habitation here to evoke this name, based on a popular but fallacious idea that ancient American Indian stocks and culture stemmed from the Valley of Mexico.

Monticello, the seat of San Juan County, is located on the east shoulder of Abajo Mountains at an elevation of 7,050 feet, the highest county seat in Utah; it was settled in 1888 from Bluff. It has been a thriving center for uranium mining and milling. The word *monticello* is Italian for "little mountain", and is the name of a town in northern Italy. There is a discrete, small mountain or hill near the town, so the name **Monticello** seems singularly appropriate. Since there were early Spanish speaking people in San Juan County, the Spanish form *Montecito* may have first been applied to the site, meaning "small mountain or wood." Or the name of Thomas Jefferson's estate in Virginia, **Monticello,** which was borrowed from **Monticello,** Italy, may have influenced the choice of name.

Monument Valley (San Juan) extends southwesterly into Arizona; Monument Pass, 5,209 feet, is on the boundary. The region is a desert plateau deep in the Navajo country; it is accessible from Mexican Hat. The region was so named from the topographic features of red sandstone mesas with sheer walls and monolithic red columns — monuments — numerous and varied. **Monument Valley** is definitely photogenic.

Moon Lake (Duchesne) is on the south flank of the Uintas in the course of Lake Fork of Du Chesne River; it is crescent-shaped which contour gave its name. It is a delightful, photogenic tarn of access from Duchesne.

Moonlight Wash (San Juan) is west of Monument Valley draining northerly into the San Juan. It derives its name from the original Navajo name *Oljeto,* "moonlight water" or "moonlight spring." A trading post near the Arizona boundary, west of Goulding's, has retained the Navajo name, *Oljeto.*

Morgan County is in the heart of the Wasatch Mountains; it embraces the Weber River Valley west of Devil's Slide to the mouth of Weber Cañon; and southerly, the historic East Cañon. **Morgan County** was organized in 1862, and named for Jedediah *Morgan* Grant, Mormon pioneer, counselor to Brigham Young, and father of the late Heber J. Grant, president of the Mormon Church. The town of **Morgan** in the Weber Valley is the county seat.

Moroni (San Pete) is a farming town in central San Pitch Valley. This name has special significance in Utah where the Mormon Church is dominant; the town was named for the Angel **Moroni** who, it is recorded, appeared to young Joseph Smith and gave him instructions in the establishment of the Mormon Church. **Moroni** is the character in the *Book of Mormon* who compiled the records of his people and others. Atop the central east spire of the LDS Church Temple in Salt Lake City, the heroic, golden-coated figure of the Angel **Moroni** with trumpet in outstretched arm publishes to millions a message of hope and peace: "Truly, the Angel Moroni symbolizes the words of the Prophet Isaiah: 'Peace, peace to him that is far off, and to him that is near'."

Motoqua (Washington) is a ranch at head of Beaver Dam Wash; it was the camp site of a Pah Ute band known as **Moquats** (Hodge).

Mount Agassiz (Duchesne), 12,460 feet, is one of a cluster of peaks of 12,000 feet range, interspersed with azure lakes, at the western end of the High Uintas; it is east of Mirror Lake. **Mount Agassiz** was named to honor Louis **Agassiz,** a famous Swiss-American naturalist.

Mount Carmel (Kane), 6,000 feet, stands on the east bank of East Fork Virgin River just north of the stream's bend to the west; it is in the lower country south of the Pink and of the White Cliffs. The roundish top of the mountain is somewhat between a cone and dome;

the form is pleasing to the eye. **Mount Carmel** was a favorite landscape subject of the western artist Maynard Dixon whose ranch home was near the hamlet of **Mount Carmel** at the mountain's base. **Mount Carmel** in the upper Virgin valley was named from **Mount Carmel** in Palestine.

Mount Carmel Junction is two miles south of the hamlet on Highway 89. This junction is the east terminus of the famous Mount Carmel Highway which wends its way tortuously from East Fork down Pine Creek to North Fork Virgin River—the floor of Zion's Cañon. Mount Carmel Highway with its tunnel and alcove windows, and the series of switchbacks providing an easy gradient to descend to the cañon floor, is a prime engineering achievement.

Mount Dutton, 10,800 feet, is the north headland of Sevier Plateau south of the confluence of East Fork and Sevier River. This prominent mountain was named by Major Powell for Major Clarence E. **Dutton** of the Geological Survey, who was the first geologist to make a scientific study of the High Plateaus of Utah.

Mount Emmons (Duchesne), 13,428 feet, southeast of King's Peak and at the headwaters of Uinta River, was named for S. F. **Emmons,** the geologist (Gannett). King, Hague, and Emmons were the geologists of the Fortieth Parallel Survey. Thirty miles to the south of the mountain, in the Uinta Basin, is the hamlet of **Mount Emmons;** splendid visibility of the mountain is afforded here.

Mount Nebo (Juab), 11,928 feet, is the dominating block of the Wasatch Range in central Utah; the Wasatch Mountains as a single chain terminate with this headland. This conspicuous mountain in the Utah landscape was named by Mormon pioneers from the highest mountain in the Biblical scene east of the Jordan in Moab, **Mount Nebo.**

Mount Terrill (Sevier), 11,530 feet, at the very source of Frémont River on Fish Lake Plateau, was named for the wife of J. H. Renshawe of the USGS.

Mukuntuweap, North Fork Virgin River drains the southern part of Markagunt Plateau and the southeastern area of Kolob Terrace; rapidly dropping into deep, grey sandstone gulches, the branches converge into **Mukuntuweap Cañon,** and the stream flows out of the cañon to join Parunuweap, East Fork Virgin River. **Mukuntuweap Cañon** is ten miles long, 3500 feet deep. This marvellously colored, awe inspiring narrow valley is the very heart of Zion National Park. Major John W. Powell explored the valley in 1871 and bestowed the original Pah Ute name—**Mukuntuweap** which, he wrote, was for "Straight Cañon." He wrote this realistic description of the Cañon: "The walls have smooth, plain faces, and are everywhere very regular and vertical for a thousand feet or more, where they seem to break in shelving slopes to higher altitudes; and everywhere are springs bursting out at the foot of the walls which are devoid of talus. The large stream bursts out from beneath this great bed of red sandstone." The Mormons named **Mukuntuweap** "Little Zion Valley."

Murray (Salt Lake), a city on Big Cottonwood Creek south of Salt Lake City, was named to honor Eli H. Murray, Utah Territorial Governor 1880-1886.

Musinia Peak, 10,986 feet, is the conspicuous southwest headland of Wasatch Plateau. From near this peak, the Muddy River drains eastward; to its south Salina Creek runs westward into the Great Basin. "Its southwest angle is decorated with a huge butte perched upon a lofty pedestal and crowned with a flat, ashlar-like block, which is a conspicuous landmark from every lofty point to the southward. This mass is called **Musinia,** and at once arrests the attention by its peculiar form" (Dutton). **Musinia** is a corruption of the Ute name of this singular peak: *Moo-se-né-ah,* "white mountain" (Lamont Johnson).

Nada (Iron) is a railroad siding on the northern part of Escalante Desert, just south of the Beaver-Iron boundary. The word is Spanish meaning "nothing"; the appellation is modern. Ten miles south of this point, the Dominguez-Escalante expedition in 1776 abruptly changed their direction, turning southeastward—manifesting abandonment of their faraway objective, Monterey.

Nasja Creek (San Juan), spanned by a natural bridge, drains northward from Navajo Mountain into the San Juan. This name and *Nesca* are corruptions of the Navajo name *Noeshja,* meaning "the owls." The natural bridge is called **Owl Bridge**—northeast of Rainbow Bridge.

Natural Bridges National Monument (San Juan) was set aside to protect three great natural bridges carved in sandstone by one meandering little stream through geologic ages; originally there were solid walls at sharp bends in the stream. These Natural Bridges are in Armstrong and White Cañons, west of Blanding. The bridges, unfortunately, have acquired dual names. English—Caroline, Edwin, and Augusta were given to these natural features by the discoverers in honor of members of their families; these names are not approved by U.S. Board on Geographic Names, and are, therefore, spurious.

"The names **Kachina Bridge, Owachomo Bridge,** the smallest of the three, and **Sipapu Bridge** were Board decisions of October 6, 1909, reviewed and the application revised in April, 1937. These names are from the Hopi language and were chosen by William B. Douglas of the General Land Office. Hopi names were assigned because of the belief that the Hopi are descendants of the people who built the cliff dwellings in the area" (USBGN).

Navajo Indian Reservation (San Juan) was established in 1884; it comprises the whole region south of the San Juan and McElmo Creek and extends into Arizona. In 1905 and again in 1933, some extensions were added north of the river, about the mouth of Montezuma Creek. The terrain is weird, in some areas marvelously enchanting. There is scant arable land, but the Navajo do cultivate some small patches; their main sustenance, direct and indirect, is from sheep and goat raising. More recently, coal, oil, and uranium ores have been found and developed on the Reservation under leases from the Navajo Tribal Council.

Navajo Mountain (San Juan) is a rugged, forbidding, giant laccolithic rock, a solitary dome with an elevation of 10,416 feet surmounting Rainbow Plateau. It is south of the confluence of Río San Juan with the Colorado River and lies mostly north of the Utah-Arizona boundary. **Navajo Mountain** is the dominating landmark of the Navajo country, and may be seen for over one hundred miles in any direction—from as far to the northwest as Brian Head, from the southwest as Cape Royal on the north rim and also on the south rim of Grand Cañon. "From whatever quarter it is viewed, **Navajo Mountain** always presents the same profile. It is quite solitary, without even a foothill for society. Its very loneliness is impressive" (Dutton). The Pah Ute named it *Tucané,* "Black Peak"; the Navajo's name of the mountain is *Na-dis*-an, "The enemies' hiding place." A. H. Thompson applied the name **Navajo Mountain** for the great Indian stock in whose country it is so conspicuous a landmark.

Needle Range extends from southern Millard through Beaver into northwestern Iron County; the Range parallels the Utah-Nevada boundary. The Range is very sharply eroded into pointed pinnacles from which feature it was named. Sawtooth and Indian Peaks are in the range in western Beaver County.

Neola (Duchesne) is a hamlet west of White Rocks. *Neo* is from the Greek *neos,* "new" and is used as a combining form in English; *la* is a locative element indicating a place, a "new place."

Nephi (Juab) is in the Juab Valley southwest of Mount Nebo; it is the county seat. **Nephi** is a progressive small city—the business center for both irrigated and dry-land farming; in the cañon to the east are rock salt quarries, plaster and flour mills; and adjacent to the town on the flat is a modern belting factory. **Nephi** was settled in 1851; the cañon stream and town were first known as *Salt Creek* from the rock salt deposits in the cañon. The old California road developed by pioneers about 1849 passed here, now Highway 91. Later, the town was named **Nephi** for one of the principal characters in the *Book of Mormon,* a prophet and a leader.

Newcastle (Iron) is a farming hamlet below the gap through which Pinto Creek emerges from the hills onto the Escalante Desert. The site was named from a slight resemblance of the abutting walls of the gap to a castle; and the element *new* was appended for euphony and as a symbol of an expected development of desert lands from impounded water in a newly projected reservoir on Pine Valley Mountains fifteen miles to the south. One alternate of the Spanish Trail emerged onto the Desert through *Newcastle Gap.*

Niatche Creek (Sevier) is a tributary of Salina Creek. This name doubtless derives from Ute. Hodge gives the Ute's own name as *No-ochi* or *Notch;* the creek's name may be a corruption of the Ute's name. *Nioche,* a ranch in the county, has for its name the Americanized form of the Ute name *No-oche.*

Ogden (Weber), county seat, Utah's second largest city, important rail and industrial center, is east of the confluence of Ogden and Weber Rivers, at the base of the Wasatch front. Near the confluence, as early as 1824, was the site of many winter rendezvous in the Great Salt Lake Valley. In 1825, three thousand traders, trappers, and Indian associates encamped for the winter here; it was first known as the Salt Lake rendezvous. It was sometimes held upstream in the mountain park, **Ogden Valley**, known then as **Ogden's Hole;** the stream was called **Ogden Creek,** both named for Peter Skene **Ogden,** factor of Hudson's Bay Company. Ogden brought his brigade from Cache Valley over the low divide to Ogden's Hole in the winter of 1824-25; American fur traders forced his retreat by the same trail. Ogden came back to Ogden Creek from the Humboldt Valley in 1828. Because of the strategic location, a gateway both north-south and east-west, the rendezvous steadily grew in importance. Miles Goodyear, about the winter of 1844-45, built a log structure at the site of **Ogden** which he called **Fort Buenaventura,** from the name of the large mythical river. The Mormon Church bought Goodyear's property in 1848. Thus, the site of Ogden may be Utah's oldest year-around white settlement. In 1850, "upon Ogden Creek, an affluent of the Weber, a city has been laid out, and called **Ogden City**" (Stansbury). The word "City" was later deleted. **Ogden** was thus named directly from **Ogden Creek,** now *River.* By extension, **Ogden Peak,** 9,575, in the Wasatch front between Weber and Ogden Rivers, was named.

Olmsted (Utah) is the picturesque hydroelectric plant in the mouth of Provo Cañon. Telluride Power Company built this power station on the Provo River in 1904; it was the first important hydroelectric development in Utah. The name **Olmsted** is that of the designing engineer; it is corrupted to Omstead.

Ònaqui Mountains (Tooele) separate Rush and Skull valleys; this range is a southern extension of the Stansbury Mountains. The name derives from Gosiute: *ó na* for "salt"; the suffix *qui* is the locative apposition (Chamberlin).

Ophir (Tooele), 6,498, is a mining camp south of Stockton in the Oquirrh Mountains. **Ophir** is the name of the principal mine, which was one of the first important gold-silver mines in the Oquirrh Range. The name is of Biblical origin, the region from which Solomon obtained gold and gems—I Kings X:11.

Òquirrh Mountains (O'queer) (Salt Lake-Tooele) extend southward from the southeast corner of Great Salt Lake; the crest is the dividing line between Salt Lake and Tooele counties. This range was an island in Lake Bonneville; and the shore terraces, on the north end particularly, sharply record the stationary levels of the Pleistocene lake. A remarkable perspective of these extinct shore lines is obtained while floating on the salt water hard by to the north. As the afternoon shadows fall, the height of the **Oquirrhs** is greatly accentuated—towering above the Jordan Valley. Bingham Cañon (q.v.) and the great open-pit copper mine are in this range.

Òquirrh Mountains are in Gosiute territory; and in pre-Causasian times the range was heavily wooded. The original Gosiute name was descriptive: *Ó pi-Ó gari,* commonly shortened to *Ó gari, Ó pi* meaning "wood or brush," and *gari* for "mountain or range," that is, "wooded mountain." An alternative meaning of *Ó gari* is "cave mountain" (Chamberlin). The present form of *Oquirrh* has been derived from the Gosiute as given through several transitional versions. There are very ancient caves in the **Oquirrh Range.** Dr. Julian H. Steward recovered human artifacts and skeletal debris from high caves which indicate an interglacial time horizon for the cave people.

Orange Cliffs are the escarpments of the surrounding tablelands through which the lower Green and neighboring Colorado River have eroded their deep courses above and below their confluence, at the foot of Still Water Cañon. The confluence is in solemn depths more than 1,500 feet below the tops of the surrounding buttes. The surface of this terrain is "naked, solid rock—a beautiful red sandstone, forming a smooth, undulating pavement" (Powell). The Utes called this region *Toom-pin wu-near Tu-weap*—a land of cañons and coves and standing rocks and buttes and cliffs and distant mountains—an ensemble of strange, grand features, weird and wonderful—"Land of Standing Rocks" (Powell). From **Grand View Point** the confluence, the cliffs, the smooth sandstone are arrestingly spread before the beholder. The name **Orange Cliffs,** bestowed by Powell, is suggestive of the color of the scarps: "A buff sandstone resting on red shale was vertical 140 feet; above this is a vertical wall of 500 feet, an orange-colored sandstone, with no breaks."

Orangeville (Emery) is a village at the east base of Wasatch Plateau, just west of Castle Dale; it was named for *Orange* Seeley, a pioneer of Castle Valley.

Orderville (Kane) is a ranch village in Long Valley. In the Mormon pioneering period when close cooperation was mandatory to survival of communities, an economic system known as the United Order was thoroughly tested here, from whence the village derived its name. In **Orderville** the United Order was eventually abandoned.

Orem (Utah), Utah's fifth city in population, 18,394, is a fast-growing, spreading community on the Provo terrace of Lake Bonneville, east of Geneva; this is a fruit-growing district and residential area for Geneva Steel workers. **Orem** was named for the builder of an electric railway which extended from Salt Lake City to Payson—now dismantled.

Otter Creek (Sevier-Piute) has its source west of Fish Lake Plateau and flows southward through Grass Valley to a confluence with East Fork Sevier River; at the confluence is Otter Creek Reservoir—one of several in the Sevier drainage. **Otter Creek** runs through the north-south dimension of Piute County—directly opposite to the flow of Sevier River. **Otter Creek** was named from the dark-brown fur bearer which inhabited the creek. The aquatic *otter* has webbed and clawed feet and lives on fish.

Ouray (Uintah) is a hamlet just above the confluence of the Duchesne and Green Rivers, below is the mouth of White River, coming in from the east; this low terrain is Wonsits Valley—the plain of the pronghorn. **Ouray** is the seat of Hill Creek Extension of Uintah and Ouray Reservation. This was formerly the Uncompahgre Ute Reservation; **Ouray** was their great chief in western Colorado. **Chief Ouray** was born in 1820; he was most friendly with the whites and spoke both Spanish and English. In the Uncompahgre homelands in Colorado, a county and its seat are named for him—**Ouray.**

Pahreah, Paria, River (Garfield-Kane) heads in Bryce Cañon, drains the east scarp of Paunsaugunt Plateau and the west scarp of upper Kaiparowitz Plateau. The stream drains southerly on the east of Pink, White, and

Vermilion Cliffs through a broad, low terrain. At the Arizona boundary the Pahreah Plateau arises; but the river evidently was there first and succeeded in maintaining its southeasterly course by eroding its channel downward into a deep cañon as the plateau arose. Twenty miles southeast, the **Pahreah River** enters the gorge of the Colorado River at the junction of Glen and Marble cañons. "The old Utah-Arizona road came down this stream for many miles. The name is Pah Ute for 'dirty water'" (Barnes, 1935).

Pahreah River, Pahreah, an abandoned post hamlet near junction of Cottonwood Creek, are in Pah Ute territory. The Pah Ute named this stream as they had Kanab Creek to the west. The hamlet **Pahreah** was settled in 1854 and named from the stream. **Pahreah** post office existed in 1883, possibly earlier, and continued to 1912 or later (Postal Guide). The name of this post office documents the original name of the river. The etymology of **Pahreah** is: the prefix *pah* is the authentic Pah Ute form for "water"; the suffix *reah* is for "dirty." The river carries a heavy burden of silt. Maps published as recently as 1934 give the name **Pahreah** for both river and plateau. The name **Pahreah** obtained for not less than eighty years. The present orthography of this name is an extreme example of corruption: how cartographers and bureaucrats have destroyed the etymology of a Shoshonean name.

Pah Vant Utes (Millard) were a favorably known band who occupied the area from Scipio on the north to Cove Creek on the south; and from the plateau on the east, these people ranged as far west as the deserts surrounding Sevier Lake. The **Pah Vants** defended this territory against other Ute to the north and east; Pah Ute to the south; and Gosiute to the northwest. They were well organized and maintained their territorial and tribal integrity until deteriorated by the whites. Their own name was **Pah Vandüts,** which meant "water people." They had many desirable village sites along the piedmont which were pre-empted subsequent to 1847 by the Mormon settlers. Their staple foods were pine nuts, berries, and roots. Trips to the House Range were made for the more palatable nut of *Pinus monophylla.* Occasional foods were deer in the mountains, water fowl along the Sevier River, and fish from the river. At Corn Creek they cultivated maize, squash, and beans.

Pahvant Plateau is the north member of the west range of the High Plateaus; it forms part of the eastern border of Millard County; a peak on the plateau east of Meadow has an altitude of 10,225 feet; Mount Catherine, east of Fillmore, is 10,082. **Pah Vant Valley** runs parallel with the plateau on its west. These physiographic features were named for a prominent Western Ute band, the Pah Vants, who occupied the region. **Pah Vant Butte**, west of Holden, is representative of several extinct volcanic craters and necks of the region which were islands in the Sevier Lake arm of geologic Lake Bonneville.

Paiute, Pah Ute, is the well-known subdivision of the Shoshonean stock who lived in the southern part of the Great Basin and bordering Colorado drainage. Hodge is authority that the name originated from *Pai,* "true", and *Ute,* "true Ute"; or *Pah,* "water" and *Ute,* hence "water Ute." Krober wrote that it cannot be considered as positively determined which of the two meanings is correct. *Piute* is a corruption of *Paiute. Pah* is a combining form in many place names of their homelands and signifies "water." There were a number of small groups of these people scattered sparsely over southern Utah, northern Arizona, southern Nevada, and even on desert areas of southern California. And to this day there are a few of these scattered groups in the area. The socio-political organization was loose or nonexistent; but the cultural elements were quite uniform throughout the extensive area. Small seeds were the characteristic food staple of the **Pah Ute** area. But the paucity of the flora and fauna of the Great Basin and bordering regions did not permit the **Pah Ute** to choose; with the exception of small patches at a few watering places, there was no agriculture; they subsisted upon the natural products of the land. The quest for food was incessant and time consuming.

Paiute Indian Reservation (Beaver) is in the Needle Range; this reservation was set aside for the **Paiute** of Beaver and Iron Counties. Indian Peak, 9,783, is the landmark for the area; and the peak is to this day the "orchard land" of the small posterity of these indigenous people as it supplies one of the native food staples—the piñon nut, Paiute *ti-ve.* In the autumn the *Paiutes* migrate from the towns to the east to harvest the large, rich nuts of the superior one-leaf piñon. The reservation has been changed to Indian Peak Game Management Area.

Panguitch (Garfield), 6,670 feet, a ranch town on **Panquitch Creek** near its junction with Sevier River, is the county seat. It is a wide custom to give a town the name of the stream on whose banks it is located. Bryce Cañon visitors and other travelers find **Panguitch** a convenient stopover point.

Panguitch Lake (Garfield), on the Markagunt near the county's western boundary, is a delightful mountain tarn; its outlet to Sevier River is Panguitch Creek. From time immemorial, native trout were prolific in this lake. This is Pah Ute territory; Pah Ute groups gathered at **Panguitch Lake** for the summers; its waters were the source of fish for a wide aboriginal area. Wootz Parashontz, my Pah Ute informant, was a member of the Cedar City group; he related that they formerly went over the snow-covered mountains early in the spring and sometimes stayed until the piñon nut season. Wootz told of their favorite way of cooking trout: without cutting or evisceration, the whole fish is placed on live coals and well heated, then the whole broiled trout is eaten.

Panguitch was the name given this lake and its outlet by the Pah Ute in pre-Caucasian times. This is an infrequent occurrence of an Indian name of a physiographic feature being absorbed into white culture with slight, if any, variation. The etymology of the word *panguitch* seems to be: the root *pangui* is similar to

Shoshonean words of wide distribution for "fish"; e.g., *pangwi, panwitci'* (Steward). The Gosiute (Shoshoni) word is very similar, *pangwitc* (Chamberlin). Parashontz gave the word for fish as *pangui.* The terminal *tch* is apparently locative—the place where.

Paragonah (Iron) is a village on Red Creek in the Parowan valley, settled in 1852; it is east of a typical Great Basin pläya—a thin sheet of brackish water—named Little Salt Lake in early American times. The Pah Ute name of this saline sheet is **Paragoon,** thus being identical with the original name given the village without the terminal *a* or later *ah:* **Paragoona, Paragoonah;** the terminal *a* or *ah* indicates a place or village—locative suffix. Frémont in 1853 used the form **Paragoona.** From the first and correct form, which preserved the aboriginal pronunciation, one *o* has been deleted, this was a bad and confusing mutilation by the Postal Service, since **Paragonah** continues to be pronounced in the aboriginal way with *oo* sound.

Paragoonah Pueblo, hard by the village, is an archaeological site of no mean importance. Not only at this site were there mounds, but along the piedmont from Paragoonah to Kanarraville early explorers and travelers counted hundreds; Captain George M. Wheeler in 1872 estimated four hundred to five hundred mounds. The Iron County Mission, which settled Parowan in 1851, observed "the remains of a town built of adobe" (Bancroft). Scientific excavations were made of what was left of the **Paragoonah Pueblo** in 1817 by Neil M. Judd of the University of Utah and the Smithsonian Institution. The mounds covered remains of rectangular, one-story, mostly adobe, communal houses. Agriculture was practiced.

Parley's Cañon (Salt Lake) and **Parley's Park** (Summit). Soon after the arrival of the Mormon pioneers in the Salt Lake Valley, **Parley** P. Pratt was directed to make important reconnaissances, such as one far to the southwest on the Spanish Trail when he verified the existence of iron ore in the Little Salt Lake region. In 1848 **Parley** explored the cañon next south of the one down which the immigrants came. He crossed the pass at the head of this cañon and found lush meadows on the highland. The cañon and meadow have since been known respectively as **Parley's Cañon** and **Parley's Park.** Highway 40 traverses the cañon.

Park City (Summit), 6,790, is on the east shoulder of the Wasatch Mountains in Weber River drainage. In 1872 a bonanza silver strike was made here which developed into the Ontario Mine; around this focus, **Park City** was built. George Gideon Snyder gave the new mining camp its name, drawing on the name of Parley's **Park** to the north. **Park City** became famous in the last quarter of the 19th century for its production of silver-lead-zinc ores; much of the wealth of Salt Lake City had its source in those mines.

Parowan (Iron), the county seat, is in the Parowan Valley to the south of Little Salt Lake. **Parowan** was founded on January 13, 1851, by the Iron County Mission. From this settlement as a base, the other four towns at the foot of the Hurricane Fault Cliffs in Iron County, and towns as remote as Bluff, and towns in southwestern Colorado and northern Arizona were colonized by parties organized here and set forth. **Parowan's** industries are farming and stock raising. The name **Parowan** has evolved from **Paragoons,** the name of the Pi-Ede band living near the **Paragoon,** the lake in the sink of the Parowan valley. This Pah Ute word **Paragoons** means "marsh people" in reference to the shores of the **Paragoon.** Early Government Indian agents and the Mormon settlers successively used **Paroan, Paravan, Parawan,** and **Parowan.**

Parowan Gap is a gulch leading from the northwest corner of the Parowan Valley through a basaltic ridge which at one time carried an overflow from Little Salt Lake. On the basaltic walls are petroglyphs inscribed by prehistoric people, possibly the Paragoonah Puebloans. Similar petroglyphs are inscribed on the basaltic walls of Cross Hollow in the hills southwest of Cedar City. Historic Pah Ute have no traditional knowledge of the inscriptions.

Pa-ru′-nu-weap (Washington) is the Pah Ute name of the gorge through which the East Fork of Río Virgen swiftly flows between Long Valley, Kane County, and the abandoned Mormon town of Schunesburgh, **Pa-ru′-nu-weap** joins **Mu-kun-tu-weap,** North Fork flowing out of Zion Cañon, east of Rockville. **Pa-ru′-nu-weap** means "Roaring Water Cañon" (Powell); *weap* is a common combining form in Pah Ute place names for cañon or watercourse. Major John Wesley Powell descended **Pa-ru′-nu weap** September 10, 1871, and bestowed the name. Dellenbaugh wrote of this trip: "The Major on foot, with a Mormon companion and a Pai Ute, explored from Long Valley down the narrow cañon of Río Virgen to Shunesburgh, about twenty miles, a trip never before made. The cañon is about two thousand feet deep and in places only twenty to thirty feet wide, twisting in such a way that the sky was not visible at times, and the stream often filled it from side to side so that they had to swim." **Paru′nuweap** is now embraced in Zion National Park.

Paunsaugunt (Pouns-a-gunt) **Plateau** (Garfield-Kane), 7,000 to 9,000 feet, parallels Bryce Cañon which has been eroded into the east escarpment of this plateau. It is drained mostly northward by East Fork Sevier River. **Paunsaugunt Plateau** is comprised largely of sedimentary sand and limestone in a tabular formation which is overlain in some areas with fairly recent lava flows. **Paunsaugunt** terminates on the south in magnificent escarpments—the **Pink Cliffs,** which in series are followed some distance to the south by the colossal terraces of the **White Cliffs,** and then the **Vermilion,** bright red to orange, all in the Colorado drainage. The margins of the plateaus have been carved by the forces of erosion thus exposing these arrestingly colored scarps. Powell characterized this gigantic terrace terrain as rivaling the Grand Cañon as a startling scenic wonderland. The name **Paunsaugunt** is Pah Ute in origin and was applied by Powell; it means "home of the beaver" (Thompson).

Payson, a prosperous town in south Utah County, is on **Peteetneet Creek** which was named for a Timpanogos Ute headman. The first name of the town was that of the creek; later, the name was changed to **Payson** to honor a pioneer townsman named *Pace*, not a reasonable derivative of his name.

Pine Valley Mountains (Washington) are a magnificent detached mountain block west of Ash Creek with an altitude of 7,000 to 9,000 feet, surmounted by Signal Point, 10,324 feet, a southern promontory. From this headland to the Virgin River bottoms at Washington is a drop of 7,324 feet; the east and south scarps are precipitous. This striking block of mountain is granitic; and, in arresting contrast to the darker, older formation, there is a high, detached basal reef or upthrust of deeply colored red sandstone around the southern end of the mountains. The name **Pine Valley** was bestowed from the heavily pine-clad, small valleys in the mountains. On the west slope, near the head of Río Santa Clara in such a valley is the hamlet of **Pine Valley.**

Pinto Creek heads north of the Pine Valley Mountains and drains northward onto the margin of Escalante Desert. **Little Pinto** is an east fork extending from Iron Mountain. A ranch on the main stream is named **Pinto.** The name derives from that of a Paiute band who occupied sites along this creek, the *Pintiats* (Hodge). The Americanized derivative **Pinto** misleads to the conclusion that the name may have derived from the Spanish word *pinto,* current in the Southwest meaning "spotted or of variegated color," applied to piebald horses, mountains, and rocks. The Spanish Trail entered this mountainous area from Cedar Valley to the east and the travelers encamped at Las Vegas de Santa Clara.

Pintura (Washington) is a fruit-growing hamlet in the narrow Ash Creek valley below the black lava ridge on Highway 91. It was settled in 1858; *Bellvue* was its former name. The word *pintura* is Spanish for "painting, picture."

Piute County, created in 1865, embraces from west to east, the east front of lofty Tushar Plateau whose crest forms the boundary between **Piute** and Beaver counties, Sevier Valley, Sevier Plateau, narrow Grass Valley, and the Parker Range; it is comparatively small in area and in population. **Piute County** was named for the well-known division of the Shoshonean stock, the **Southern Paiute**. The form of the name adopted by the Legislature is divergent from those approved by ethnologists; **Paiute** and **Pah Ute**, the ordinary pronunciation is Pī-yūt′.

Piute Creek in **Piute Cañon** (San Juan) heads south of the Utah-Arizona line and drains northward east of Navajo Mountain into Río San Juan. **Piute Creek** has been the eastern boundary of Pah Ute territory from pre-Spanish times; they shared a part of this region with the Navajo who probably came into the area considerably later. The form **Piute** is a corruption of **Paiute**.

Plateau Province: In the region of the junction of the Green and Colorado Rivers, "The country was a vast plateau similar to the one through which the Cañon Desolation is carved, that is, tilting northward and increasing in altitude toward the south, so that as the river runs on its cañons become deeper from this cause as well as its cutting. These great terraces terminate on the south in vertical cliffs—through which the river emerges abruptly. From such features as these the Major named this the **Plateau Province**" (Dellenbaugh). "The southern escarpments of these cliffs are a series of gigantic and complicated terraces or steps. Occasionally high buttes and mountain masses arise from the surface, but generally the area of the Basin of the Colorado River is a plateau country—a land of mesas, cliffs, and cañons" (Dellenbaugh).

Pleasant Grove (Utah) is at the west base of Mount Timpanogos. Near a small stream flowing from Timpanogos a sanguinary skirmish occurred in March, 1849, between Mormon settlers and Utes who had been marauding the white man's livestock. This was the first "formal" episode in Utah which was so typical of the conflict between whites who pre-empted the homelands of the aborigines and the latter's retaliation in stealth. The stream became known as Battle Creek—a name common across America connoting bloodshed between the indigenous people and the permanent invaders. A Mormon town was built near the creek and given its name. Later, the settlers changed the harsh name to the more mellow **Pleasant Grove.**

Portage (Box Elder) is a village west of a shoal in the Malad River just south of the Utah-Idaho line. The word is French and means "to carry"; **portage** had wide usage in French-Canadian domain both as a verb and as a noun, the latter indicating a place over which canoes and stores are carried from one stream or lake to another, or around a cascade or shoal in a stream, such as exists here in the Malad. The name was applied by Hudson Bay's trappers in the 1820's.

Price (Carbon), the county seat and largest town in eastern Utah, is in the Price River valley on the east slope of Wasatch Plateau; it is the focal point of the coal-mining industry. **Price** was named from that of the river on whose banks it is located; this is a common mode of toponymy. There is a folklore story about the origin of the name **Price** which the credulous relate.

Price River (Carbon-Emery) arises on the crest of Wasatch Plateau and flows southeasterly into the Green River. **Scofield Reservoir** is across the channel near the stream's source. **Price River Cañon** from Colton to Castle Gate, eroded in grey sandstone, is most scenic. The name **Price** was bestowed on the river for an early pioneer, William **Price** who settled in the valley.

Promontory (Box Elder) is a hamlet northwest of Brigham City in the low terrain between the north and south sections of the Promontory Mountains. The south section is a long rocky peninsula, first named **Promontory Point,** jutting southward into Great Salt Lake west of Bear River Bay. The word *promontory* means a high rocky headland projecting into the sea. Near the hamlet is a monument marking the site of completion of the first transcontinental railroad. "Promontory Summit was the name specified by Congress as the location at which the two railroads (Union Pacific, extending west 1,086 miles from the Missouri River and the Central Pacific, extending eastward 690 miles from Sacramento) were to join their tracks. This name was shortened to Promontory in Central Pacific timetable, and that name continued after Southern Pacific tracks were torn up in 1942." The Golden Spike ceremony took place on May 10, 1869. In the Union Pacific station, Salt Lake City, is an heroic mural painting depicting the engines of the two roads approaching and Governor Leland Stanford driving the Golden Spike into a special hole prepared for it in the laurel tie with a silver-headed maul.

Provo (Utah), east of the mouth of Provo River, is the county seat and is Utah's third city in population, 36,047. The city was named directly from *Provot River*. Howard Stansbury, U.S. Eng., in his report (1852) of reconnaissance survey of Great Salt Lake, relates that in the spring of 1849 "a settlement was commenced, and a small fort built near the mouth of the Timpanogos, an affluent of Lake Utah, about fifty miles south of the city" (Salt Lake City); ". . . which is to be called **Provaux City.**" Even though *Provo* derives from French, this was an erroneous elaboration of the orthography. Another corruption, **Provost City,** was used in 1854, the French surname evidently having been confused with the military title *provost marshal.* The name of the city was later corrected by omitting the *s,* and simplified by dropping the *t,* to *Provo,* and the word *City* was deleted, as has occurred in the names of many Utah towns. "City of Provo was founded in 1850, eastward of Fort Utah, at base of Wasatch Mountains, where timber and pasture were abundant, and where the gradual fall of the Timpanogos affords excellent water-power" (Bancroft, 1889). **Provo** is the home of the fast expanding Brigham Young University, and is the social and business center of Utah County.

Provo River, Provo Cañon, Upper Valley (Utah-Wasatch). **Provo River** is the principal affluent of Lake Utah; its source is Washington Lake in the western Uintas; after descending the south slope of these high mountains, its course is through the undulating **Upper Valley** meadowland in Wasatch County; below Deer Creek Reservoir, it drops into **Provo Cañon** to pass through the Wasatch front south of Mount Timpanogos, thence southwesterly to debouch into the lake. The aboriginal name of this stream was **Timpanogos** for "rock river"; and after **Provot** became the name of the river, the name *Timpanogos* was transferred by whites to the mountain.

The name **Provo** is for Etienne **Provot,** not "Provost," and the *t* is silent, a famous French-Canadian explorer and *voyageur*. Dellenbaugh wrote that Etienne **Provot** was called *l'homme des montagnes,* "the man of the mountains." Not even Kit Carson or Jim Bridger was more familiar with the dangerous Far West than was **Provot.** Etienne **Provot** was in the **Upper Provo** and other Utah valleys as early as 1825 (Alter). His rendezvous was most often in the upper valley of the Timpanogos; and this Indian name of the stream gradually changed to **Provot River.** The only lasting change since was the dropping of the *t,* and that entailed no change in pronunciation. **Etienne Provot,** explorer and *voyageur,* is commemorated in the group of figures on the east façade of "This is the Place" monument in the mouth of Emigration Cañon.

Pruess Lake (Millard) is just south of Garrison in Snake Valley within two miles of the Nevada border. This lakelet was named by Captain John C. Frémont for Charles **Pruess,** cartographer of his first two expeditions.

Quitchupah Lake (Iron) is just within the Great Basin—at the base of Iron Range southwest of Cedar City; it is a typical Basin pläya. Near where intermittent Leach's Spring empties into this brackish sheet, there is a natural bedding ground for mule deer and for pronghorn antelope. The etymology of the word *quitchupah* is: *quitchup* is Pah Ute for "dung"; the suffix *pah* for "water," that is, "bed ground, watering place." **Quitchupah** is an excellent example of a Pah Ute place name, with known etymology, being adopted into white culture. The Spanish Trail threaded up Leach's Cañon from this lake, thence to the Mountain Meadows.

Rainbow Bridge National Monument (San Juan) was set aside in 1910 to protect Rainbow Natural Bridge, "the greatest of all known natural bridges, a symmetrical arch above and below" simulating the arch of a rainbow. This magnificent arch spans Bridge Cañon on the northwest slope of Navajo Mountain, ten miles downstream from the confluence of the San Juan River with the Colorado. This extraordinary natural bridge, whose arch in form and coloring is strongly suggestive of a rainbow, is 309 feet above the stream bed and has a span of 278 feet. The great natural wonder is an example of the effect of stream erosion—one geologic explanation being that the arch was formed through the penetration by the stream of the neck of an entrenched meander—oxbow. The Pah Ute name of the bridge is *Barohoini,* "the rainbow"; the Navajo name is *Nonne-zoshi,* "great arch"; thus, the English name parallels the Pah Ute. In 1909, John Wetherill, Dean Byron Cummings, and W. B. Douglas were the first white men to view **Rainbow Natural Bridge.** Currently, a controversy rages as to how the Reclamation Service should engineer the protection of **Rainbow Bridge** against the waters of Lake Powell.

Rainbow Plateau, 6,000 feet, is an elevated domed area south of the San Juan in Utah and Arizona; it is the most inaccessible, least known, roughest area in the Navajo Reservation. **Rainbow Plateau** is characterized by bare red rock beset with closely placed cañons, and natural bridges abound. Navajo Mountain arises 4,000 feet above the general level. By extension, **Rainbow Plateau** was named from Rainbow Natural Bridge.

Randolph (Rich), the county seat, is a ranching community in the Bear River Valley. This town was named for **Randolph** H. Stewart, supervisor of its founding. There was an early Mormon trend to give towns and counties the given names of locally prominent persons.

Red Cañon (Daggett) is the Green River channel after it is deflected due eastward by the Uintas, clearing Bear Mountain at a right angle. Major Powell named it from the color of its walls. He named the rapids in **Red Cañon** Ashley Falls for General W. H. Ashley. Flaming Gorge Dam is being built in **Red Cañon.**

Rhodes Valley (Summit), 6,500 feet, is an important physiographic feature in that it separates the north-south trend Wasatch Mountains from the west-east trend Uinta Mountains. The upper Weber River, with branches heading in the Uintas to the east, flows northward through the high valley toward Coalville. **Rhodes Valley** was named to honor Thomas **Rhodes,** a pioneer rancher.

Rich County embraces the northeast corner of Utah, being a long, narrow area extending northward from Echo Cañon. The southern half of Bear Lake is in **Rich**; the northern half, in Idaho. **Rich County** was organized in 1864 and named for Charles C. **Rich,** an early Mormon apostle, who was prominent in the settlement of the Bear Lake region.

Río de la Virgen, Virgin River, a tributary of the Colorado River, has two main originating Forks: the East Fork drains Long Valley in Kane County; the North Fork drains the south escarpments of the high Markagunt Plateau and undulating Kolob Terrace in Iron County, then cuts its deep course down through Zion Cañon to a confluence with the East Fork east of Rockville. There are two other north tributaries not far to the west: La Verkin Creek drains Kolob Cañons; and Ash Creek drains the Hurricane Fault Cliffs and adjacent valley from Kanarraville southward. Southwest of Pine Valley Mountains, Río Santa Clara joins **Río Virgen.** Heavily laden with silt, the river flows southwesterly, south of Saint George, out of Utah.

Río de la Virgen, the original form of the name, is pure Spanish, literally, "River of the Virgin," that is, dedicated in name to the Virgin Mary. Antonio Armijo headed a large party of Spanish traders who succeeded in traversing the region between Santa Fé, *Nuevo Mexico,* and the *Mission de San Gabriel* in *Alta California,* January 31, 1830. Armijo was the first Spaniard to bridge the two Mexican provinces, but it is not clear that he bestowed the name on this river. Yet the Spanish name, *Río de la Virgen,* adhered for a century and was the first form in recorded history. The Spanish Trail prevailed from *circa* 1830-1850 between Santa Fé and Pueblo de los Angeles. There are to this day existent Spanish natural feature names along the entire route, which argues without refutation that the River was named by the Spanish who gave it a most characteristic Spanish-Catholic name—*Rio de la Virgen.* It required over one-half century after American sovereignty of the region to Anglicize the name to Virgin River.

Río Santa Clara, Santa Clara River (Washington) has originating branches on the Pine Valley Mountains; it makes a sweeping crescent curve, first to the west and south, and at Shivwits turns to the southeast to a confluence with Río Virgen south of Saint George. "*Río Santa Clara* was an important link in the Spanish Trail to southern California. The Trail left the west side of Cedar Valley through a pass in the Iron Range and reached the *Río Santa Clara* south of a well-known place named by the Spaniards Las Vegas de Santa Clara" (Bancroft's *Utah*). Franciscan padres, who explored the Spanish Trail, dedicated the stream to *Santa Clara de Asis.* This sweet saint was the founder of the order of Franciscan nuns known as the "Poor Clares"; *Santa Clara's* symbol is the lily (Sanchez).

Río San Rafael, San Rafael River, Valley (Emery). **Río San Rafael** has its source in Huntington, Cottonwood, and Ferron Creeks high on the east slope of Wasatch Plateau, above Castle Valley, and drains southeasterly; in its lower course the stream makes a graceful curve directly eastward through **San Rafael Valley** to join Green River. Powell described the drainage basin as "woefully barren and desolate." The Old Spanish Trail proceeded due west from the Gunnison Crossing to the north shoulder of San Rafael Swell, thence up the river to ascend the Wasatch Plateau. Franciscan friars dedicated this river to *San Rafael Archangel,* "the angel of the spirits of men"; he was also the "healer." The name *San Rafael* was popular and bandied about in the nineteenth century.

Saint George (Washington), the county seat, is in the lower Virgin Valley on H. 91. This attractive town was founded in 1861; its industries are farming, stock raising, and tourist business. The town was thus named to honor **George** Albert Smith, counselor to President Brigham Young of the Mormon Church. President Young maintained a winter home in Saint George so as to enjoy the mild winter climate; his house still stands in good condition and is a tourists' attraction. **Saint George** is the site of the first of four LDS Temples to be built in Utah. The structure is of black lava and red sandstone—both closely available; the walls are covered with stucco painted snow-white causing the magnificent building to shimmer in the "Dixie" sunshine for many miles. Dixie College, a state junior college, is located here.

Saint John (Tooele), a hamlet in Tooele Valley, was named for *John* Rowberry, a pioneer of Tooele. **Saint John** and Saint George illustrate one mode of Mormon town naming.

Salduro (Tooele) is a Salt Desert railway station near the Bonneville Salt Flats, the automobile speedway. **Salduro** is a modern appellation formed from Latin elements: *Sal* for "salt"; and *duro,* "hard"; that is, "hard salt." *Salduro* is a Spanish word of equivalent meaning. An immense bed of rock salt about sixty miles long and eight miles wide is in this area of the Great Salt Lake Desert.

Salina (Sevier) is an historic town in the Sevier Valley at the junction of **Salina Creek** with Sevier River. The early Spanish name of the creek on whose banks it was founded was given the town by successor people—the Mormon colonizers. This is an excellent example of a natural feature name, creek, being bestowed first, then much later a town being given the name. Santa Clara and Las Vegas, Nevada, are parallel examples.

Salina Creek (Sevier) heads on the crest of Wasatch Plateau and drains westerly down **Salina Cañon** to a confluence with Sevier River in the valley. There are deposits of rock salt in the Cañon with adjacent salt seeps. The Spanish Trail, after crossing Green River at the Gunnison Crossing, followed up Río San Rafael to near the site of Castle Dale; thence it treaded southwesterly, beyond the site of Emery, to upper branches of the Muddy River flowing eastward, and found a cañon leading to a pass at 7,923 feet over the crest of Wasatch Plateau; the Trail was then in the Great Basin drainage as it descended **Salina Cañon.** Utah Highway 10 follows this natural route from Castle Dale to Salina. The Spaniards named the creek from the salt seeps: *Salina* (sah-leé-nah), the Spanish word for "a salt marsh or pond." *Salina* is one of the pure Spanish names in Utah which was absorbed into American culture. Its pronunciation has degenerated. In California the name is plural—*Salinas.*

San Francisco Mountains (Beaver) are northwest of Milford. These mountains were named for *Saint Francis of Assisi,* founder of the Franciscan order of which *Friars Dominguez y Escalante* were members. It is probable the name was applied in reference to the 1776 expedition headed by them which passed this district southward. **Frisco,** a defunct mining camp in these mountains which centered about the Horn Silver Mine, was named with a corrupted form of **San Francisco.**

San Juan County was created in 1880; it is the largest county in Utah—an immense domain having an area of 7,761 square miles in the southeast corner. Its northern boundary is common with Grand County; its western bounds are the Green and Colorado Rivers; on the east is Colorado; on the south, Arizona. The topography of **San Juan** is most varied, and in many areas weird and inaccessible. Running from east to west in its southern section is the **San Juan River** from which the county was named.

San Juan River, Río San Juan, Río San Juan Bautista, the latter is the full Spanish form of the name, "Saint John the Baptist River," and is of frequent occurrence in Spanish America. The headwaters of **Río San Juan** are in the **San Juan** Mountains of southwestern Colorado and northwestern New Mexico; the main stream heads near Farmington, New Mexico, and courses northwesterly into Utah a few miles north of Four Corners, thence generally westerly across San Juan County. In its lower courses the San Juan has carved a deep box cañon with many entrenched meanders, and enters the gorge of the Colorado in Glen Cañon. **San Juan** is a name common to contiguous sections of three states: New Mexico, Colorado, and Utah. There are two explanations of the origin of the name **San Juan River:** 1) In 1598 the Spanish under Don Juan de Oñate undertook the conquest and settlement of *Nuevo México.* Oñate possessed the Tewa pueblo *Caypa* on the east bank of Río Grande del Norte north of Santa Fé as headquarters of the provisional Spanish government; he renamed the Indian pueblo **San Juan,** to honor himself, by which name it has since been known. By extension, the name was supposed to have been applied to the mountains to the northwest and the river flowing from them. 2) According to J. J. Hill, it is possible **Río San Juan** was so named by *Friars Dominguez y Escalante* in honor of Don Juan María de Rivera who in 1765 explored northwest from Santa Fé to what is now known as the Gunnison River.

San Pete County was organized as one of the original eight when Utah Territory was created by Congressional Act in 1850. The Territorial Legislature corrupted the aboriginal name to this form, which may readily be mistaken for a corruption of "Saint Peter." **San Pete County** includes **San Pitch Valley** and its watersheds.

San Pitch Valley, Creek, and **Mountains** are west of the Wasatch Plateau in central Utah. The Creek runs southerly down the Valley, thence westerly to join Sevier River near Gunnison. The **San Pitch Mountains,** the west wall of the valley, with elevation of 9,000 feet, are much lower and less rugged than the Wasatch Plateau, the east watershed, with an elevation from 10,000 to 11,300 feet at South Tent. **San Pitch Valley** is one of Utah's rich agricultural and thickly populated valleys. The name of these physiographic features derived from the name of the Ute division whose homelands embraced this area, and who were known by several variant names: *Sampitches, Sampichya, Sampiches,* and *Sanpuchi.* "They wintered in the Sevier River Valley where there was less snow and where they could take deer, rabbits, ducks, and geese and trap beaver and mink."

San Rafael Swell (Emery) takes its specific name from that of Río San Rafael. The generic term *swell,* rather rarely used, is given to a rise of or undulation of the land. **San Rafael Swell** is a widely known physiographic feature of the Green River region; it is a great anticlinal uplift of the rocks of all the geologic formations of the Colorado-Utah region—even to the underlying igneous granite. On the east of this elongated dome, the sharply upturned sedimentary rocks form a gigantic table tilted to the east, and this has been serrated by the streams cutting many notches in its surface. Surmounting the **Swell** near its center, is an irregular elevation called **San Rafael Knob,** 7,934. The eroded, notched surface of **San Rafael Swell** is the physiographic base of a gorgeously sculptured landscape. Viewed from Gunnison Crossing, it is especially beautiful when silhouetted against the horizon at sunset. As the sun descends below the horizon, a fantastic spectacle of buttes, pinnacles, turrets, spires, castles, gulches, and alcoves develops, which is known in eastern Utah as "the Silent City."

Santa Clara (Washington) is a fruit-growing village on the banks of **Río Santa Clara;** by extension, it was named from that of the river. And twenty-five years before the village was founded by Mormons, the river was named by Spaniards from Santa Fé, it being an important link in the Spanish Trail. Jacob Hamblin, the Mormon scout in the Colorado Basin, built one of his well-distributed homes here in 1853; it is currently an historic show place. A fort was built in 1856.

Santaquin (Utah) is south of Lake Utah; near the site a sanguinary skirmish occurred between Mormon settlers and Indians under a Ute named **Santaquin;** the growing village then adopted his name. The highway forks west of **Santaquin:** 91 extends southward; 6-50 leads westerly via Eureka and Delta to Ely, Nevada.

Scipio (Millard), settled in 1860, was first known as Round Valley from the contour of the valley in which it is located east of Cañon Mountains. At the suggestion of Brigham Young, the name was changed to **Scipio,** after the great, popular Roman General, Publius Cornelius **Scipio,** Africanus Major, who defeated Hannibal, which event lead up to the destruction of Carthage by Africanus Minor.

Scipio Peak, 9,719, and South Mountain, 9,231, are in Cañon Mountains which extend northerly from Pavant Plateau; Scipio Cañon separates these two ranges, and Highway 91 traverses the cañon and pass. The Dominguez-Escalante party in October, 1776, treaded the same route, sans highway; an historic marker commemorating this event stands in a turnout near the pass. The Cañon Mountains are dissimilar to the Pavant Plateau in that they are comprised of non-conformable strata—resultant from much agitation in the mountain-building process. **Scipio Peak** is an extension of the name of the village.

Sevier County is one of seven through which Sevier River flows; by extension, the county was named from that of the river. **Sevier County** extends from San Pete on the north to Piute and Wayne on the south; and from the crest of Pah Vant Plateau on the west to a south-north line on the east, which is roughly along the east front of Fish Lake Plateau and the southern end of Wasatch Plateau. All three of these plateaus were geologically described as such by Clarence E. Dutton (1880). The Sevier River courses through the county from the hamlet of Sevier on the south, northeasterly to Redmond; its valley is rich in agriculture and well populated.

Sevier River, Río Severo, has its source in the extreme southeastern part of the Great Basin; its headwaters share the drainage of the High Plateaus of southern Utah with branches of Pahreah River, Kanab Creek, and Río Virgen, all of which latter streams flow in the opposite direction into the Colorado River. **Sevier River** flows northward for nearly two hundred miles through comparatively high and narrow valleys between the High Plateaus of Utah; the current is quick; the climate, brisk. The river makes a grand curve to the west in southern Juab County, rounds Cañon Mountains, thence trends southwesterly in Millard County; and, after forming several extensive deltas in the flat terrain, formerly emptied into the thin sheet of the same name—**Sevier Lake,** now dry. **Sevier Lake,** so called, is one of the largest of the Great Basin pläyas. Sevier Desert extends northward from the deltas. Areas comprising Lake and Desert were in Glacial times a considerable part of extinct Lake Bonneville. **Sevier River** is the longest Great Basin river wholly within Utah. The volume of water does not vary much throughout the river's course.

Sevier River in name, similar to the names of the Green and Virgin Rivers[1], has its genesis in the original Spanish name *Río Severo.* Explanations of the origin of the names of these three rivers have been based on insufficient research of pertinent historical data, and there has been shallow striving for plausibility and un-

[1]Rufus Wood Leigh, "Naming of the Green, Sevier, and Virgin Rivers," *Utah Historical Quarterly,* April, 1961.

warranted authority. Folklore has displaced history. Spanish explorers from the *Río Grande del Norte* as early as 1813 named this river *Río Severo.* In the journal of Antonio Armijo, citizen of Santa Fé, who bridged the two Mexican provinces of *Nuevo México* and *Alta California* in 1829 via *El Vado de los Padres,* is mentioned the Spanish name bestowed on our river, *Río Severo.* T. J. Farnham detailed the exploration of an old trapper down *Río Severe,* using an equivalent American descriptive word. In 1848 Frémont wrote: "Southwesterly from Lake Utah is another lake; it is the reservoir of a handsome river about 200 miles long. The river and lake were called by the Spaniards, *Severo,* corrupted by the hunters (Americans) into *Sevier.*" In the "Report of Expedition of E. F. Beale in 1853" is the following: "July 31, 1853 . . . *Sevier* is the corruption of *Severo.*" By this time there had been many American trappers and traders in the region; and now there were the Mormon settlers. The bent of Americans was to simplify and corrupt both Indian and Spanish place names.

Shivwits Indian Reservation is a sizeable square area in southwestern Washington County, including a narrow strip of arable land in the Santa Clara valley, and extending westward onto the Beaver Dam Mountains. In this Reservation, Highway 91 makes the difficult and extra-mileage bend up the Santa Clara and over the pass. A new water-level route has been surveyed from near Washington down the Virgin River; in the Virgin gorge across the Arizona border, the roadbed will be carved from solid rock.

Shivwits is in the narrow valley on the Reservation; it is the *rancheria* of the remnant of a Pah Ute band whose habitat originally included the **Shivwits Plateau** to the north of the Colorado River in Arizona. These few people were brought from their homelands and placed on the Santa Clara River where the government aids and encourages them in agriculture and livestock. The meaning of the root of the name, *Shiv,* is undetermined; the suffix *wits* is for "people."

Skull Valley (Tooele), southwest of Great Salt Lake, lies between the Stansbury Mountains on the east and Cedar Mountains on the west. **Skull Valley Indian Reservation,** set aside for Gosiute and Shoshoni, is in the southeast part of the valley. This valley was crossed from west to east by the Hastings party on May 30, 1846—truly a trail-blazing journey. They named it Spring Valley "because of its abundant water and broad stretches of meadow" (Stookey). This route around the south shore of Great Salt Lake became known as the Hastings Cutoff. The name Spring Valley did not come into usage; the present name became popular in the early 1850's. As to the origin of the name, a myth became current that the Gosiute "buried their dead in a large spring in the valley, and that skulls found floating in the spring gave the valley its name" (*ibid.*). This was not a Gosiute mortuary practice. Folklore creates false explanations of the origin of geographic names, it is here exemplified at its best. Dr. Stookey's research indicates that H. Severe and J. McBride, the first settlers of Grantsville, gave the valley its name because they found *buffalo skulls* some six feet deep in the alluvial soil where water had cut deep gullies; no buffalo skulls were ever found on the surface. Buffalo skulls were also found in the soil in Rush Valley, south of Tooele Valley.

Silver Reef (Washington) is Utah's famous ghost town; it had a population of 10,000 in 1875. The site is northwest of Leeds, near the southeast base of Pine Valley Mountains. The geologic formation of the district is reefs of red sandstone. The singular occurrence of silver in sandstone was found here; a vein of silver in sandstone is unique. The word *reef* is the name of an upthrust or cliff of rock, and these reefs bore veins of silver. Several silver-bearing reefs had been given the names of their respective discoverers. A name was sought for the whole district: a distinctive name for the West's latest bonanza camp; **Silver Reef** was proposed and adopted. Exploitation of the reefs depleted them of silver in the early 1880's; population migrated; structures deteriorated.

Skutempah Creek is a north tributary of Salina Creek; this is Ute territory. The etymology of the name is: *skutem* is for "rabbit brush"; *pah,* "water"; hence, a creek with rabbit brush growing along its banks.

Spanish Fork (Utah), a stream having its source high in the Wasatch Mountains, issues down a cañon of the same name and is the second affluent of Lake Utah. The specific name **Spanish** derives from the fact that the Dominguez-Escalante expedition in 1776 followed down this stream into Utah Valley; and more particularly, this cañon was the main route of the Old Spanish Trail into the Great Basin from 1830-1850, and it was also an alternate route of the Spanish Trail to *Pueblo de los Angeles.* The generic term *fork* was in popular usage in the West in referring to tributaries of rivers and affluents of lakes; this usage was parallel with that of "run" and "branch" on the Atlantic seaboard.

Spanish Fork, a Mormon city settled in 1850, is located southeast of where the **Fork** debouches into Lake Utah. This application is an example of the mode of naming a town with that of the stream on whose banks it is located. Most physical features of Utah were named prior to 1847, other than survey place names.

Spanish Fork Cañon is the natural and historic route from Utah Valley to eastern Utah and Colorado: it follows the Spanish Fork drainage to Soldier Summit, 7,477, where it crosses the Great Basin-Colorado River divide into Price River drainage. The Denver and Río Grande Western Railroad and Highway 6-50 traverse this route.

Spanish Fork Peak, 10,185, north of the Cañon in the Wasatch front, was so named by extension.

Spanish Valley (Grand), 4,000, drains northwesterly to the Colorado River south of Moab. The Spanish Trail diverted westward from Río Dolores, traversed low passes south of Sierra de Sal, thence northwesterly down this low altitude, pleasant valley to the Colorado crossing. There were many caravan encampments in this green, cottonwood vale, and from these associations the valley was so named.

Springville (Utah), settled in 1850, is a prosperous small city southeast of Provo. The community was named for a large warm *spring* which issues from the base of the Wasatch in Hobble Creek Cañon east of the town; the naturalized suffix, *ville,* is for "village." The spring unfailingly supplies pure water for fish hatcheries in its stream bed. **Springville** is noted for its Art Institute; it is the residence of large highway contractors.

Stansbury Mountains (Tooele) are between Tooele Valley on the east and Skull Valley on the west; in their southern section, Deseret Peak attains an altitude of 11,031 feet. A detached, northern section juts into Great Salt Lake from the south as a rugged, peninsular island; from Salt Lake City, the far west horizon is formed by this promontory, in summer sunsets it looms large. These mountains were named for Howard **Stansbury,** Corps of Engineers, who headed the first government survey of Great Salt Lake in 1849-50.

Still Water Cañon (Wayne-San Juan) of the Green River is south of Labyrinth; it has scarped the Orange Cliffs above the confluence of the Green and Colorado Rivers. Powell gave this name because of the low gradient and slow current of the Green which attains great depth in this cañon—from 2,000 to 3,000 feet. **Still Water** is 42.75 miles in length (Powell) and ends at the confluence.

Stockton (Tooele) is a mining village at the west base of the Oquirrh Mountains south of Tooele. Rich mineral deposits were found here in the 1870's by the California Volunteers under the Command of Colonel P. E. Conner. Figuratively, the name was transplanted from **Stockton,** California.

Strawberry River rises east of the Wasatch Mountains—east of Utah Valley—and flows eastward to join Duchesne River at Duchesne. Highway 40, passing over Daniel's Cañon Summit at 8,000 feet, southeast of Heber, enters the high, well-watered **Strawberry Valley.**

Abundance of wild strawberries grew in this swampy valley from which it was named and, by extension, the river. **Strawberry** is a widely applied geographic name.

Strawberry Reservoir (Wasatch) is a sizeable man-made lake; it was formed in the south end of **Strawberry Valley** by a dam built across the stream bed by the Bureau of Reclamation. This project is an unusual engineering feat in that the impounded water is drained off through a tunnel in a direction opposite to the river's flow. The tunnel was bored under a low divide to the southwest, its west portal is at the head of Diamond Creek which is a north branch of Spanish Fork. Thus, the waters of **Strawberry River,** which is in the Colorado River drainage, have been impounded, diverted by tunnel, natural stream beds, and canals to irrigate farm lands in southern Utah Valley in the Great Basin. **Strawberry Reservoir** is well stocked with game fish.

Summit (Iron) is a farming hamlet seven miles west of Parowan; **Summit** was so named because of its location on the crest of an upland between the Parowan and Cedar valleys, with an elevation of 6,130 feet—the highest community on Highway 91 in Utah.

Summit County was created in 1854. **Summit** was chosen as the name because the county embraces high mountain areas which form the divides between the Weber, Bear, and Green River drainage areas. It includes the crest of the Wasatch, east of Salt Lake and Morgan counties, the Rhodes Valley of the upper Weber River, and from the crest of the High Uintas northward to the Wyoming line and eastward to Daggett County.

Tabby Mountain (Duchesne), 10,000, is an outlier butte south of the Uinta Mountains, just west of the upper Duchesne River. **Tabby Mountain** was named for a famous Ute chief; the meaning of the name is undetermined. "For a brief period the Ute were organized into a confederacy under a chief named **Tabby** (*Taiwi*)" (Swanton). **Tabiona** is a hamlet on the Duchesne to the east of the mountain. To the name of the mountain the locative case ending *ona,* indicating a place, has been affixed.

Tantalus Creek (Garfield) is a branch of Frémont River. The name is from Greek Mythology: **Tantalus** was a wealthy king who was punished for an atrocious sin by being placed in a lake whose waters receded whenever he attempted to allay his thirst. The word *tantalus* is the root of our verb *tantalize.* Many Southwestern creeks recede for a major part of the year. A. H. Thompson applied this name, doubtless due to disappointment in the recession of the creek.

Terrace Mountains (Box Elder) are off the northwest shore line of Great Salt Lake, their highest elevation is 7,028 feet. They were thus named by Howard Stansbury on October 29, 1849, during his survey of the lake shore, when he observed shore lines of extinct Lake Bonneville; he counted thirteen discrete terraces—marking shore lines of considerable duration.

Thermo (Iron) is a railroad siding on the northern Escalante Desert. The word *thermo* is from Greek *therme,* "heat" and is used as a combining prefix in many technical terms, signifying "heat or hot." The name of the station was adapted from **Thermos Springs** nearby; this name was applied to these hot springs by USGS.

Thousand Lake Mountain (Wayne), 11,295, is east and north of Frémont River. The mountain has many lakelets scattered over its surface; from this feature, it was so named by Major J. W. Powell.

Timpanogos, Mount (Utah), 11,750, is the most magnificent block in the Wasatch Range, commanding as it does the entire Lake Utah drainage. The eastern aspect is truly Alpine. The name is a variant of the aboriginal name of the river flowing at the south base of the mountain; and also is the name of the indigenous people who lived on the shores of Lake Utah, known in the *Yutä* tongue as *Timpanogo* (Escalante Journal). *Timpanogo* is Ute for "Rock River," and by the Indians was originally applied to the American Fork and Cañon; later, by some, to the Provo River (Dr. R. V. Chamberlin). After **Provot** became the name of the river, the name **Timpanogos** was transferred by whites to the mountain.

Timpanogos Cave National Monument was named from the mountain on whose north slope, in American Fork Cañon, the limestone cave is located.

Tintic Mountains—East and **West** (Juab), with intervening **Tintic Valley,** are typical Basin ranges north of the big bend of the Sevier River; **Tintic Mountain,** 8,214, due west of Mona, is the highest peak. These mountains and valley were named for a Western Ute chief, **Tintick,** who, according to Armstrong (1855), was a chief at Lake Utah. Gottfredson (1919) described the Gosiute as a band living in Cedar, **Tintic,** and Skull valleys under Chief **Tintic,** a "renegade chief." By extension the famous **Tintic Mining District** in these mountains was given the name as was also **Tintic,** a mining camp southwest of Eureka.

Tooele is the seat of Tooele County; this thriving small city is at the west base of the Oquirrh Mountains in the eastern part of Tooele Valley from which it was named.

Tooele County was one of the original eight created in 1850. **Tooele** is one of Utah's large counties: it embraces the major part of Great Salt Lake Desert, southwest part of Great Salt Lake, Skull and Tooele valleys; it extends from Nevada eastward to the crest of the Oquirrh Range; and from Box Elder on the north to Juab County on the south. **Tooele County** was named from Tooele Valley.

Tooele Valley extends southward from the most southern tip of Great Salt Lake; Oquirrh Mountains are on its east, Stansbury Mountains, on the west. The unusual Stockton Bar, at the south end of the valley, was thrown across a pass connecting Tooele bay with the smaller Rush Valley bay by oscillation of the waters of Lake Bonneville. In aboriginal times there was rank growth of several species of rush in both these valleys. Several explanations, some folklore, have been given as the origin of the name **Tooele.** In Gunnison's

History of the Mormons is the following: "In Tuilla valley, thirty miles west of the temple, is a settlement." *Tule,* a word of Aztec origin, is a large variety of the common great bulrush, *Scirpus occidentalis,* common in marshes and lakes in the West. *Tule* grows in the marshes of the valley today. Gudde writes that "*tule* derives from the Aztec *tullin* or *tollin*; the word designates the bulrush or similar plants with sword-like leaves, as shown by an Aztec symbol . . In Spanish exploratory times the word *tule* was used descriptively." The slough in **Tooele Valley** would have been so described. The Spanish pronunciation of *tule* (too′-le) is suggestive of the spelling as given by Gunnison and others then current. *Tuilla* could not be derived from the Gosiute (Shoshoni) word for tule, *saip.* It is related that Brigham Young's scribe, not knowing the current orthography of the valley's name, *Tuilla,* spelled it as it sounded to him: **Tooele,** which corruption has since been perpetuated. Thus, the name is traceable back through Mormon and Mexican corruptions to its ultimate Aztec origin.

Topaz Mountain (Juab), 7,113, is a semicircular mountain of greenish rhyolite—an intrusive rock—in the Thomas Range. The semiprecious stone *topaz* is found in this mountain. *Topaz* is translucent and of several clear hues; it has been a prized stone from ancient times. During War II a detention camp for 8,200 Japanese nationals called **Topaz** was located south of the mountain.

Toquerville (Washington) is an interesting, fruit-growing village on lower Ash Creek; the site is on broken terrain at the base of an upland composed of sedimentary sandstone capped with an overlay of black lava. The name has evolved through several forms: **Tokar, Toker, Toquer, Tokerville,** and **Toquerville.** *Toker* or *Toquer* are versions of the Pah Ute word for "black." The author tested this word with several Pah Ute informants. *To-quo* is Ute for "black mountain." Considering the relation of the village site to the black upland, *toquer* is the root word. The suffix *ville* is "village"; **Toquerville** is thus a hybrid compound—from Pah Ute and English. *Toker* was also used as the name of a Pah Ute headman by whites; his camp site on Ash Creek was pre-empted by Mormon settlers. The Southern Indian Mission wrote under date of 22 June, 1854: " . . on Ash Creek, or the Upper Río Virgen, found Chief Toker's present home. They (Indians) were clearing land at the base of the mountains on the eastern side of the river. We saw corn, squashes, beans, watermelons." This is a validation of aboriginal horticulture. "*Pa-spi-kai-vats* is the name of the Pah Ute 'band' which lived in the vicinity of Toquerville, a district on lower Ash Creek" (Isabel T. Kelly).

Trachyte Creek (Garfield) drains the northern slope of Mount Hillers in the Henry Mountains and flows into the Colorado River at Hite. *Trachyte* is the name of a light-colored, rough, volcanic rock, mainly feldspar. The Creek courses through beds of trachyte and was so named by A. H. Thompson, June 20, 1872.

Tremonton (Box Elder) is a prosperous agricultural town on the Malad River; this river was trapped by Hudson's Bay Company men during the trapper era—1820-39. These French-Canadians left several place names along this stream, **Tremonton** may have been one of them. The etymology of the word is: *tres,* "three"; and *monton,* "heap or hill." There are three low peaks in the vicinity. Or, the town's name may be a transfer from that of **Tremont,** Illinois, made by a group of settlers from there in 1903; but the determinant in both cases was the proximity of the three peaks.

Tushar Plateau (Beaver-Piute) crest forms the rugged boundary between these counties. Because of their tabular structure, C. E. Dutton, eminent government geologist, who was the first to study the High Plateaus of Utah, places **The Tushar** as the middle member of the west range of the High Plateaus. He describes them in accurate, beautiful English (1880): "Two noble cones ending in sharp *cusps* stand preëminent: Belknap and Baldy which reach above timber line and are very striking on account of the light cream color of their steep slopes and the ashy-gray of the apices—carved by erosion out of the vast block of the tabular mass; these are the grand pyramids of Belknap and Baldy. The Tushar dip to the west with gentle sloping foothills; the east front—facing the Sevier Valley—is high and sharply steep." The word *tush,* a noun, has the same meaning as *tusk,* one meaning of which is, a sharp, projecting, tooth-like *cusp.* The adjective form, **Tushar,** was applied as the name of these mountains, descriptive of the high sharp peaks. **Mount Belknap,** 12,139 feet, was named for William Worth Belknap, Secretary of War under President Grant; **Delano Peak,** 12,173 feet, was named for Columbus Delano, Secretary of the Interior under Grant; **Mount Baldy,** 12,000 feet, the name is descriptive of its barren area above timber line.

Uinta Basin is the large west-east depression which flanks the southern side of the Uinta Mountains. Erosion of the Uintas supplied the sediments laid down in the **Basin.** "The Uinta Basin is a natural depression lying in northeastern Utah and northwestern Colorado. It comprises all of Duchesne and Uintah counties, Utah, the western half of Río Blanco, and the southwest corner of Moffat County, Colorado. All the principal drainage is into the Green River" (G. E. Untermann). **Unita Basin** was the original homelands of the *Uinta,* Yampah, and lesser divisions of the Utë Indian stock; the **Basin** was named for the Uinta Utës.

Uinta Mountains are the highest range in Utah; there are several 13,000-foot peaks. The **Uintas** are unique in that they are one of the largest west-east trending ranges in the Western Hemisphere. They extend from Rhodes Valley, east of the Wasatch Mountains, eastward to the Utah-Colorado boundary and northward to the Wyoming boundary. Structurally, the **Uintas** were formed by a broad arching of the earth's crust; this broad, anticlinal uplift was subsequently eroded into its present forms. The **Uinta Mountains** are in contrast to the Basin ranges which are tilted monoclinal blocks.

Uinta River has its source south of King's Peak in the High Uintas, flows southeasterly to a confluence with Du Chesne River south of Randlett, Uintah County. **Uinta River** was named very early in Caucasian times for the **Uinta** division of the Utë Indians.

Uintah (Weber) is a railroad station and farming village at the mouth of Weber Cañon which was settled in 1850. The site received its present name March 4, 1867, when the Union Pacific Railroad was finished to this point (Bancroft). This is outside the territory of the Uinta Utës, a misapplication of the name.

Uintah County was one of the original eight organized in 1850; it then embraced the areas now included in Duchesne and Daggett counties. It is a long rectangular domain extending southward from the crest of the Uinta Mountains to a common boundary with Grand, in the eastern tier of counties. The county was named for a division of the Utë Indians. *Uintah,* a variant of *Uinta,* is applied to political entities, whereas *Uinta* is applied to natural features and to the *Uinta Utës.* The form *Uinta* is a contraction of *Uintats,* a division of the Utë living in northeastern Utah (Hodge). Gannett writes that the word means "pine land." An early form of the name was *Euwinty.*

Uintah and Ouray Indian Reservation is a long west-east area at the foot of the Uinta Mountains in Duchesne and Uintah counties, extending from Stockmore to Tridell. "President Lincoln proclaimed a large part of the Uinta country an Indian reservation on the third of October, 1861." It was intended that the populous Utë be protected in their ancestral rights against white squatters. The Utë inherited the Uinta country from their remote ancestry and brooked no intrusion of whites. Without consulting the male tribal members, as was inherent in the original treaty, Congress enacted legislation opening the **Uintah Reservation** to homesteaders in August, 1905, which, as

G. E. Untermann writes, "was a shameful episode in the government's dealings with the American Indian." The present reservation is a mere remnant, composed largely of the "bad lands" of the Uinta Basin, of their former homelands. Later, Uncompahgre and other Utës from western Colorado were shunted by government decree onto the reservation with the Uinta Utës, hence the addition of the name **Ouray** (*q.v.*).

Yutäs, Utës, Utahs, Utes. The Utës are a principal subdivision of the Great Basin-Plateau Shoshonean stock, and they with the Aztecs of the Valley of Mexico form the great Uto-Aztecan linguistic family. The first written reference to them is in Fray de Escalante's journal as *Yutäs* (1776). English quivalents followed in the first half of the next century. *Utës* was a widely used early form of the name; its singular, *Utë*, was pronounced *Yoo-tah,* and thus the aboriginal pronunciation is preserved in the state name **Utah**; the two words were used interchangeably (Steward). **Utah** is derived from that of the *Utë* or *Uta* tribe; all the various forms *Uta, Utah, Yoo-tah, Eutaw,*[1] *et al,* are synonymous with the present name of this Shoshonean stock, **Ute** (Hodge). Thus, there has been a corruption in the pronunciation of **Utë** to **Ute** (Ut) in the current name of these people. Western Colorado, eastern and central Utah, constituted the main habitat of the **Utë** Indians. Swanton (1953) gives the entire range of the Utës as stated above and also includes the eastern part of Salt Lake Valley, Utah Valley, and extends into the upper drainage of the San Juan River in New Mexico. Early in Caucasian influence the Utës adopted the horse culture, were expert hunters, were better nourished and clothed than such neighbors as the Pah Utes, and developed considerable tribal cohesion with accompanying social practices—made possible by the horse. The Utës had no agriculture.

Utah Lake, Utah Valley, Utah County. The Dominguez-Escalante expedition, attempting to find a way over the *tierra incognita* between Santa Fé in*Nuevo México* and Monterey on the coast of *Alta California,* were the first Europeans to enter the region which is now Utah. Their longest encampment was made on the eastern shore of Lake Utah; and the entries then made in their journal were rich and full. The padres named the lake *Laguna de Nuestra Señora de la Merced de Timpanogotzis*" (Bancroft). They named the Indians whose villages were about the valley, *Lagunas,* "Lake People." The journal records that other bands of *Yutäs* called these people at the lake *Timpanogotzis.* Escalante also used the Indians' own name for the lake, *Timpanogo.* The principal river of the fan of tributary streams was likewise known as *Timpanogo.* Dominguez called the Indians of the whole region *Yutäs,* just as the Indians themselves pronounced it.

May 24, 1844, Captain John C. Frémont came north from *Río Severo* into Utah Valley and encamped on the bottoms of the Spanish Fork. He recorded: "The principal river is the *Timpanogo* signifying 'Rock River'—a name which the rocky grandeur of its scenery, remarkable even in this country of rugged mountains, has obtained for it from the Indians. . . . restricting to the river the descriptive term *Tim-pan-ogo,* and leaving for the lake into which it flows the name of the people who reside on its shores (*Utës*), and by which it is known throughout the country." Thus, the name of the lake confirmed by Frémont became firmly established—**Utah.** By extension, the valley and later the county both acquired the same name, and all three names preceded the naming of Utah Territory. The descriptive name of the river, *Timpanogo,* which he also approved, did not adhere, as at this date (1844) it had been known for two decades on its upper reaches as the **Provot River** (*q.v.*).

Utah Territory, State, name derived from the Indians' own name of themselves. The first recorded form was Spanish by Fray Francisco Dominguez when the expedition of 1776 was encamped on the shores of Lake

---

[1]The form *Eutaw* was used by Washington Irving (1837) in his "Bonneville."

Utah—*Yutäs.* The English versions *Utës, Utahs, et al* followed in early 1800's. The true Indian pronunciation as indicated in the Spanish *Yutä* and English *Utë* and *Utah* is preserved in the State name. The word means, according to Gannett, "home or location on the mountain top." Prior to 1848, the larger region of which the settled part of Utah was encompassed was known as Great Basin, North America. After the treaty of Guadelupé—Hidalgo, February 2, 1848, the permanent settlers, the Mormons, gave the name of **Provisional State of Deseret** to an extensive domain. **Deseret,** the name signifying "honeybee"[1], included all of the present Utah and Nevada, and parts of Oregon, Idaho, Wyoming, Colorado, New Mexico, Arizona, and California, with San Diego as a Pacific port. The **Provisional State of Deseret** obtained legally from 1848 into 1850; in that year the Congress organized **Utah Territory,** the Organic Act was signed by President Millard Fillmore on September 9, 1850. In 1861 the Territory of Nevada north of the 37th Parallel was carved from the Territory of Utah; and in 1862 and again in 1866 an additional degree of Longitude was ceded by the Congress to Nevada bringing Utah's west boundary to 114° West Longitude. Utah was admitted to statehood January 4, 1896, as the forty-fifth state.

Vernal is the seat of Uintah County, the principal town in Ashley Valley, and the focal point of oil development in northeastern Utah. The State Museum, the Utah Field House of Natural History, is in **Vernal.** This is a most creditable institution which has been developed by G. E. and B. R. Untermann. Superb collections of physical and biological specimens and ethnological artifacts recovered in the Uinta Basin are displayed; and, in particular, there are well-articulated dinosaur skele-

[1] "And they did also carry with them Deseret, which, by interpretation, is a honey-bee; and thus they did carry with them swarms of bees" (*Book of Mormon,* Ether 2:3).

tons from nearby Dinosaur National Monument. **Vernal** was settled in 1879 and first named **Ashley** for General William H. Ashley of fur trade fame in the 1820's. The name was changed to **Vernal** in 1893. The English *vernal* means belonging to spring; also, pertaining to youth. The word stems from Latin through French *vernalis,* a most attractive name for a growing community.

Vernon (Tooele) is a ranch hamlet in the southern end of Tooele valley. **Vernon** is an English surname, a favorite Christian name, and a common American place name. The hamlet was named for Joseph **Vernon,** a founder.

Veyo (Washington) is a hamlet on the upper Santa Clara River. Though the word *veyo* may appear Spanish, it is actually a Mormon synthetic word—a masterpiece —composed in sequence of the initial letter of the following words: virtue, enterprise, youth, and order.

Wah Wah Mountains are a desert range in western Millard and Beaver counties. **Wah Wah Valley** is parallel with the mountains on the east; it is a southern extension of Sevier Lake playä; water collects in the valley's sink after storms but is soon evaporated in the arid atmosphere leaving a salty or alkaline plain. *Wah Wah* is from the Pah Ute tongue, signifying "salty or alkaline seeps."

Wales (San Pete) is a hamlet southwest of Moroni; it was settled by Mormon immigrants from **Wales;** and the colonizers named their new home in memory of the ancient Celtic country, a part of Great Britain. In contrast, most people in the county are of Scandinavian origin.

Wanship Peak (Summit), 9,308, on the west side of Weber Valley, was named for a Salt Lake Valley Shoshoni. **Chief Wanship** was living in the Salt Lake Valley in 1845; he told Captain Frémont that he could ride on horseback to Antelope Island in Great Salt Lake. By extension, a hamlet and reservoir on the Weber are named **Wanship.**

Wasatch County is an irregular area of high altitude—on the top of the **Wasatch Mountains** from which it is named. In the well-watered meadowlands of the Upper Provo, Etienne Provot held his rendezvous with trappers, traders, and Indian associates during the trapper era; and today this valley is the home of the main population of **Wasatch County.** Highway 40 traverses the county from the northwest to the southeast up Daniel's Cañon.

Wasatch Mountains are one of the dominating ranges of the continent. Their peaks range in elevation from 9,000 to nearly 12,000 feet above sea level. During the glacial epoch this range supported a number of glaciers. The structure is monoclinal, with an original vertical fault escarpment on the west and a gentler incline on the east. The **Wasatch** form part of the east rim of the Great Basin. The **Wasatch Mountains** terminate at about Mount Nebo in central Utah; from that latitude southward, there are three ranges of High Plateaus (*q.v.*). The combined chain forms the chief physiographic feature of Utah; along its western fertile piedmont are most of the settlements. *Wasatch* is Utë, it refers to "a low pass over a high mountain range."

Wahsatch (Summit), 6,850, a rail station and a pass between the Weber and Bear River drainages, at the head of Echo Cañon, is a perfect application of the Utë word **Wahsatch.**

Washakie (Box Elder) is a small Indian Reservation on the Malad River south of Portage. **Washakie,** chief of the Wyoming Shoshoni, induced temporary peace toward the whites; he was a remarkable personality with persuasive power. He maintained amity with white transient immigrants and with white settlers (Steward). This site was one of his camps. **Washakie** is commemorated among the figures on the east façade of "This is the Place" monument at mouth of Emigration Cañon.

Washington (Washington) is an historic town on **Río** Virgen six miles east of St. George; it was founded in 1857—four years before St. George was settled. Historically, **Washington** is noted for its pioneer factory in which serviceable cotton cloth and other products were fabricated; the lava stone building stands in good condition today. The town was named from the county.

Washington County, organized in 1852, encompasses the southwestern corner of Utah—the Río Virgen drainage. The altitude of arable and habitable parts is about 3,000 feet, the exposure is mostly southern, which result in a warm, equable climate, permitting the cultivation of cotton, sugar cane, grapes, and other fruits in pioneer days. In consequence of these crops the county early acquired a nickname: Utah's "Dixie." Today, turkey raising is an important industry as is catering to tourists. **Washington County** was named to honor President George Washington; the name was selected when the Legislature was considering providing a block of Utah marble to be placed in the Washington Monument.

Wayne County is roughly a long parallelogram extending from Piute County on the west to Green River on the east; Sevier and Emery counties are on the north; Garfield on the south. The principal physiographic features, from the west to east, are: Awapa Plateau; northern part of high Aquarius Plateau; to its north is Thousand Lake Mountain; Frémont River flows southerly to near Bicknell, then, bisecting the high plateaus, runs easterly to Hanksville, thence southeasterly to the Colorado; east of the plateaus are Capitol Reef and Water Pocket Fold; beyond, the terrain is lower to Green River which moves through Still Water Cañon. **Wayne County,** organized in 1892, was named for the son of William E. Robinson, member of the Legislature.

Weber County, one of the original eight, embraces the drainage of Ogden River, a magnificent section of the Wasatch front, and the plain extending westward to Great Salt Lake through which the lower course of Weber River, after being joined by Ogden River, meanders to debouch into the lake. The county was named from Weber River.

Weber River, Cañon, is the second largest affluent of Great Salt Lake, its headwaters are to the southeast in both the Wasatch and Uinta Mountains. **Weber Cañon** together with its northeast fork, Echo, is the main gateway into Utah, having the lowest altitude through the Wasatch; it early became the route of explorers, trappers, immigrants to the Far West, Union Pacific Railroad in 1867, and modern Highway 30s. In 1825 a detachment of Ashley's men headed by John H. **Weber** explored and trapped down the river's narrow valley. Weber was one of four of William Sublette's men who circumnavigated Great Salt Lake in 1826. In the winter of 1828-29, John H. Weber was killed by Indians near the river. Sublette, factor of the Rocky Mountain Fur Company, named this important stream **Weber River** for his fallen man.

Wellsville (Cache) is a farming town in southwest Cache Valley; it was settled in 1856 by Peter Maughn and named to honor Daniel H. Wells, Commander of the Nauvoo Legion, a military organization continued from the former Mormon city in Illinois.

Wendover (Tooele) is a Western Pacific Railroad station around which a stopover point on Highway 40 has developed; the station is on the western edge of Great Salt Lake Desert on the Utah-Nevada line. The name is a modern appellation, a compounding of the verb *wend* and the adverb *over*—suggestive to betake one's self over the flat, broad Salt Desert.

West Tavaputs Plateau (Carbon) is west of Desolation Cañon of Green River. The tableland has a general elevation of 8,000 feet, surmounted with strips of 9,000 and peaks of 10,000. Powell applied the name for a Ute headman of the region. To the southeast, across the Green River in Grand County, is a plateau of lesser elevation named **East Tavaputs Plateau.**

White River, Río Blanco (Uintah), has its source in northwestern Colorado, flows westward into Utah to join Green River in Wonsits Valley near Ouray. The Dominguez-Escalante expedition of 1776 crossed the Colorado River near the site of De Beque, Colorado, crossed over Roan Plateau and got into Douglas Creek drainage which brought them down to the **White River** which they crossed where the oil town of Rangely is now located. They named the mother stream *Río San Clemente*. Later Spanish explorers named the river *Río Blanco,* "White River," so named because of the white cliffs forming its cañon walls. This Spanish name is perpetuated in Colorado as the name of the county through which *Río Blanco* flows—*Río Blanco County.* As history unfolded, **Río Blanco** was Americanized to **White River.**

Whiterocks River flows southerly from high in the Uintas east of Uinta River and joins that stream in western Uintah County. The name was chosen from the color of rocks in the stream's course. Just above the confluence is the seat of the Uintah and Ouray Indian Reservation, the most important Ute center, **Whiterocks,** named from the river. This Agency was established Christmas day, 1868. It is the oldest site of continuous settlement in the Uinta Basin. Major Powell on his exploratory trip down the Green River in 1869 left the river and walked over to **Whiterocks** to mail letters.

Wonsits Valley (Uintah) is the open flat plain where the Duchesne, coming in from the northwest, and the White River, coming in from due east, make confluence with Green River. *Wonsits Yu-av* is the Ute name of this valley. *Wonsits* is Ute for "antelope"; in aboriginal times the pronghorn ranged in large bands on this level plain. *Yu-av* is Ute for "flat or level." **Wonsits Yu-av** and Gunnison Valley, south of Book Cliffs, are the only open plains onto which Green River emerges from its somber cañons.

Yampa Plateau (Uintah), 8,335, is a prominent tableland northeast of the Jensen crossing of Green River and extends south of the Yampa River in Colorado. By extension, the plateau was named from the river; the river was named from the *yampäh* plant which grows in its valley. The Yampa River drainage was the habitat of a distinct band of Utës—Yam Pah Utës—whose favored food was the roots of the *yampäh.* Frémont, while exploring in the Yampa valley, noted: "The Utës considered the *yampäh, Anethum graveolens,* the best among the roots used for food. It was a staple and particularly abundant in the Yampah River Valley."

Zion National Park is a rich scenic gem in the dissected Río Virgen country in eastern Washington County. The very heart of **Zion Park** is the gorge—narrows—and the deep cañon southward of the North Fork. East Fork of Río Virgen, coursing westward from Kane County, joins the Zion Cañon stream south of the park entrance. The Indian names of these two streams were applied by Major John W. Powell in 1872: **Mukuntuweep** was the Pah Ute name of North Fork and its awe inspiring narrow valley; **Parunuweep** was the aboriginal name of East Fork. Powell was the first white man to thread down the narrow gorge of **Parunuweep.** The etymology of these two names is given separately (*q.v.*). Local Mormon settlers had explored **Mukuntuweep** and farmed small plots on its flat bottoms from 1858. They named it "Little Zion," "Little" being used to offset any detraction from central Zion—Salt Lake City. **Mukuntuweep Cañon** became a National Monument in 1909. In 1918, the monument was changed in name to **Zion** and enlarged; the next year it attained the status of **Zion National Park** by Act of Congress. **Zion** rapidly attained national repute as a cañon of rare grandeur in formation and color, and of a magnitude to be encompassed by eye and mind of lovers of nature's masterpieces. In 1923 President Warren G. Harding with a large entourage paid a visit to **Zion National Park.**